T H E

ENGLISH GARDEN

TRADITION

THE
ENGLISH GARDEN
TRADITION

DAVID JOYCE

CENTURY

London Melbourne Auckland Johannesburg

First published in 1987 by Century Hutchinson Ltd, Brookmount
House, 62–65 Chandos Place, Covent Garden, London, WC2 4NW

Century Hutchinson Australia Pty Ltd
PO Box 496
16–22 Church Street
Hawthorn
Victoria 3122
Australia

Century Hutchinson New Zealand Limited
PO Box 40–086
Glenfield
Auckland 10
New Zealand

Century Hutchinson South Africa (Pty) Ltd
PO Box 337
Bergvlei
2012 South Africa

Set in 11/12pt Palatino by AKM Associates (UK) Ltd, Ajmal House,
Hayes Road, Southall, London UB2 5NG.

Separated, printed and bound in Singapore through Print Buyers' Database

British Cataloguing in Publication data

Joyce, David
  The English garden tradition:
  learning from the great gardeners of today
  1. Gardening – England
  I. Title
  635′.0942   SB453.3.G7

ISBN 0 7126 1761 2

This book was designed and produced by The Paul Press Ltd,
41/42 Berners Street, London W1P 3AA

Art Editor	Mike Snell
Project Editor	Elizabeth Longley
Picture Researcher	Vicky Walters
Art Director	Stephen McCurdy
Editorial Director	Jeremy Harwood

To my mother and father

Some explanation is needed of the hybrid formula – neither fully literary, nor a word-for-word
record of conversation – I have used to present the material covered in the interview or
interviews with each of the contributors. The transcripts of the taped conversations provided
startling evidence of my readiness to be entertained by amusing anecdotes, or to deflect
conversation in the direction of personal interests in plants and gardens. By the time I had
edited out my guilty attempts to get conversations back on course, there seemed little point in
my voice being heard at all. I hope that a tighter and more fluent text makes up for the loss of
an authentic conversational tone that has resulted from removing the voice of the interviewer
and for the adjustments I have made, particularly to the ordering of material. It has to be
stressed that the texts are edited interviews and that the contributors, who include writers of
considerable distinction, might have approached the subjects they deal with in very different
ways if they had been asked to write rather than to talk about them.

Contents

The English Garden

A delight in gardens and in plants is far from being a uniquely English preoccupation. The water-cooled elegance of Moorish courtyards, the subtle miniaturization of Japanese landscapes and the grand symmetry of the French traditional style all reflect a deep pleasure in gardens, although the form of expression differs greatly from culture to culture. The English, however, have a long-standing reputation as passionate and accomplished gardeners, which is justified by the number and quality of beautiful and interesting gardens that are open to the public. If current statistics of leisure activities are to be believed, the tradition is very much alive.

This book brings together contributions by ten knowledgeable gardeners, each *talking* about – for the chapters are based on edited interviews – a particular aspect of garden design or planting. It is my hope that, as well as being interesting and informative about specific topics, the composite effect of these contributions conveys something of the character of English gardening, even British gardening, although the limited scope of the book is intentional.

The character of English gardening
This eludes precise definition but some general points about it can be made. As a starting point, the country's climate and geology are factors that cannot be ignored. The limitations they impose can be overcome by the creation of artificial environments – heated glasshouses, for instance, in which tropical plants such as pineapples might be grown – but the native tradition of gardening is moulded by the fluctuating temperatures of the changing seasons and the quality and characteristics of the soil.

Visitors to England often comment on how unpromising the climate seems to be for gardening. However, for those of us who are accustomed to its moist variability (drier and sunnier but often colder in the east, milder and wetter in the west) it is not without compensations. There are moments of fugitive but rare beauty, often in defiance of the weather forecast. And there is a soft light, lingering on long summer evenings, that enhances subtle harmonies of texture and colour and in which pale shades glow with a luminous intensity. At their most sophisticated, English gardeners have exploited this hazy and often feeble light as a wonderfully fluid medium to intensify a palette of gentle colours.

As plants are not uniformly hardy, climate determines what can be grown in the open, but the impoverished native flora of Britain gives

The success of many English gardens rests on a sensitive combination of formal elements and a wealth of 'cottagey' plants. In this corner of the garden at Barnsley House in Gloucestershire, box cones and box hedges provide a permanent green framework for a planting in which herbs play a leading part.

little indication of the astonishingly wide range of plants from all parts of the temperate world that *can* be grown successfully here. Perhaps the very limited range of native wild plants in part explains the appetite for new introductions that has been a striking feature of English gardening since the Elizabethan period.

Along the western seaboard, where the warming influence of the Gulf Stream is felt from Cornwall to the north of Scotland, gardens can include numerous tender plants that in severe conditions could not survive without protection in inland and eastern parts of the country. However, the chances of a succession of mild winters or, more importantly, springs where there are no wild fluctuations of temperature, is a strong temptation to many gardeners to grow marginally hardy plants in particularly favoured sites. In a climate of more certain harshness the risk would not be justified. Not surprisingly, therefore, great value is put on a garden with a favourable aspect, gently sloping (so that frost will drain away) and south-facing, enjoying a sheltered position and benefiting from features such as warmth-retaining walls.

The record of triumph and failure in this gamble with the vagaries of the climate is of absorbing interest to many gardeners.

Turf grows well in the moist and relatively mild climate of Britain so that the management of good-quality lawns is much less troublesome than it is in many other countries. Long before the invention of the mechanical cylinder mower, in 1830, the fineness of English lawns was commented on by foreign visitors; since the seventeenth century at least areas of close-mown grass have featured prominently in English gardens. Indeed, devotion to the lawn, as travelling through suburban London by train reveals, may have been carried to an extreme. It is as though the ideal of velvet perfection in the mind's eye of the owner miraculously cancels out what can be a scruffy and unsightly reality. The more imaginative use of hard surfaces in small gardens is probably a very healthy development.

The physical character of the English landscape has profoundly influenced the tradition of English gardening. When William Kent 'leaped the fence, and saw', as Horace Walpole wrote, 'that all nature was a garden', he was looking on a gently undulating, rarely dramatic, landscape of rural calm. The eighteenth-century landscapists were certainly sensitive to the 'genius of the place'. But the intention of professionals such as Kent and amateurs of genius such as Henry Hoare, the creator of Stourhead, was not simply to heighten the landscape's own character. The purpose of their remodelling – which included the damming of streams to form lakes, the planting of screening belts of trees and carefully arranged clumps, the elimination of regularity and symmetry in favour of undulating contour and sinuous line, and the addition of architectural incidents – was to charge the landscape with classical resonances. We are no longer well-equipped to appreciate their landscapes as they intended. That their inspiration was classical, although sometimes filtered through the vision of painters such as Claude and Poussin, is to us less important than their poetic quality, which over the years has come to represent an ideal of Englishness.

The most important geological factor affecting gardening is the acidity or alkalinity of the soil. Although many lime-loving plants will grow satisfactorily on neutral or even acid soils, acid-loving plants – in particular rhododendrons – will not tolerate lime. However, F.C. Stern's classic, *A Chalk Garden*, will give heart to any gardener with a limy soil for in it he tells how at Highdown, on the south side of the Downs, near Worthing, he made a garden of exceptional quality from a barren chalk pit. A successful chalk garden can be infinitely more cheerful than some of the large woodland gardens planted on acid soil early this century, where the overwhelming preponderance of rhododendrons provides a hectic display in the flowering season followed by months of lugubrious sullenness.

Unique heritage

The landscape movement of the eighteenth century has been enormously influential in the history of the English garden, almost as much for what it has swept away as for what it has contributed. But neither it nor any other style represents uniquely the English tradition.

Yew hedges and yew trees clipped to shape provide the living architecture of many old English gardens. At Great Dixter in East Sussex the yew topiary and hedges were planted early this century but they seem to harmonize perfectly and complement the splendid fifteenth-century manor house.

We are extremely fortunate that gardens reflecting almost every tendency and influence of the last four hundred years can be seen in Britain, particularly, although not exclusively, in the properties owned and managed by the National Trust.

In the tug of war between formality and informality, almost all the architectural gardens of the seventeenth century have been destroyed but there are some fine reconstructions in which axial symmetry, regular shapes and geometric patterns dominate the design in the style of that period. A good example is the knot garden at Ham House, where the scheme – based on a plan of 1670 – consists of box-edged beds tightly planted with cotton lavender arranged in diagonals, with the corners and mid-points accentuated by box pyramids. Another example in the seventeenth-century style is the Queen's Garden at Kew, interesting not only for the design but also because the planting has been restricted to what was in cultivation prior to 1700. True to the spirit of the period, an artificial mount – in this case built from an accumulation of cinders and ashes from old glass-house boilers – gives an opportunity to admire the garden's architectural quality.

The showy formality, with bedding-out plants arranged in the parterre designs that were fashionable in the Victorian period, is a style so costly in terms of labour that it is now almost something of the past. What made it possible were technical developments in heated glass-houses and the availability of many new tender or half-hardy plants, which in a protected environment could be raised in great numbers for planting out when required. Vestiges of these schemes survive in municipal planting programmes and in some large gardens, but the once frequent changes of bedding are now generally reduced to two, one for spring and another for summer.

Dutch, French and Italian influences are discernible in many phases, particularly as the inspiration of formal garden arrangements. At Hampton Court, for example, the radiating avenues, grand canal and formal parterres were executed in the grand French manner for William and Mary by the Brompton Road nurserymen, London and Wise, this scheme obliterating Cardinal Wolsey's great garden. But here, as in so many other gardens with a long history, the process of evolution – for a garden is always changing – has softened the late-seventeenth-century scheme. An attractive feature of many of England's great gardens is that the evidence they reveal of shifts in fashion and style does not detract from – but rather contributes to – the highly individual character of the amalgam.

9

What is sometimes now held against the formal style of the eighteenth century is that the reworking of the landscape was generally so radical that it has obliterated all traces of earlier schemes. At Blenheim Palace, for example, the original scheme by London and Wise, a magnificent garden in the grand French manner surrounding Vanbrugh's baroque masterpiece, was almost totally destroyed when 'Capability' Brown remodelled the landscape in the 1760s. It is often considered his finest achievement but the creation early this century of new parterres, including on the west front elaborate water parterres, is a kind of judgment on Brown's 'eternal green' formula.

A taste for the exotic and romantic is another theme recurrent in English gardening. More often than not the exoticism is simply expressed in the addition of architectural features, for instance, in the oriental style, as the Pagoda at Kew. But the 'picturesque' landscapes of the nineteenth century called for a more coherent treatment. One of the most delightful successes in this style is Scotney Castle in Kent. In the 1830s, the owner, Edward Hussey, decided to have a new mansion built in an elevated position above the moated cluster of old buildings (including a fourteenth century tower) and to reduce these to form a romantic ruin. What had been a damp and inconvenient home became the focal point of a magically evocative landscape.

Formality versus informality

In the late nineteenth century the sometimes absurd debate between proponents of formal and informal styles of gardening sharpened. The most vociferous opponent of formality, particularly of the 'pastry-work gardening' of bedding-out, was William Robinson, whose highly influential book *The English Flower Garden* was published in 1883. His rejection of the excesses of Victorian formal gardening went hand in hand with an enthusiastic championing of hardy plants and a genuine appreciation of their particular qualities. In this he was picking up a theme that John Claudius London had already aired at the beginning of the Victorian period.

There is no single style of gardening that can be described as uniquely English, but what shows through in the best of the English tradition is a deep love of plants and flair in combining them. The way you rank them will depend very much on your own priorities.

It is a curious irony that the most influential gardener in the Robinsonian tradition should be Gertrude Jekyll, for here was an exceptionally knowledgeable plantswoman with an artist's eye achieving some of her greatest successes within the formal schemes of Edwardian country houses that she worked on in collaboration with the architect Edwin Lutyens. Many of the finest gardens of the twentieth century are a synthesis of informal planting of great richness within a formal framework. The best-known examples are the garden created by Major Lawrence Johnston at Hidcote Manor in the Cotswolds, and Sissinghurst Castle in Kent, made by Vita Sackville-West and her husband Harold Nicolson.

For many gardeners, now as in the past, the debate between formality and informality is quite unreal. The task is rather to find the place or places in which various plants will grow best and therefore be presented in the best possible way. To be described as a plantsman or plantswoman is for many gardeners the highest compliment to connoisseurship in plants, based on practical experience of growing them successfully.

Specialist gardens
A mixture of scientific curiosity, imperialism and a desire for good garden plants culminated in the nineteenth century in a flood of introductions on such a scale that specialist gardens were created to accommodate them. On a grand scale there were arboretums and pinetums for trees, such as the Westonbirt Arboretum in Gloucestershire. For rhododendrons there were woodland gardens such as those created by the Loder family in Sussex, of which Leonardslee is the most celebrated. An enthusiasm for alpines and other small plants led to the building of giant, even monstrous, rock gardens. The interest in alpines and rock plants continues unabated but the great accumulations of rock assembled in the late nineteenth and early twentieth century have proved difficult to manage and it is mainly in large public gardens, such as Edinburgh and Kew Botanic Gardens, where they continue to function as settings for these small plants.

A specialist interest in plants is nothing new and nor is its combination with a taste for competition. It is a mixture that can be seen at every level of gardening, from vegetable growing to rivalry over roses. Its most touching expression was in the cultivation by artisans, particularly in the eighteenth century, of the old florists' flowers (that is flowers bred for perfection of bloom, not, as in the modern sense, flowers for decoration) such as auriculas and carnations.

The English gardener's love of plants is, perhaps, the right note on which to end this introduction. It radiates from so many modest gardens, even little balconies. It rescues many a formal garden from banality. It supports a considerable nursery trade, at its best more interested in satisfying a customer with a good plant than in making a large profit, and it is fostered by numerous general and specialist gardening organizations. It has also given rise to a literature that ranges from works of scrupulous scholarship to endearing expressions of personal pleasure in plants and gardens. The contributors to this book all bear witness to the English gardener's love of plants.

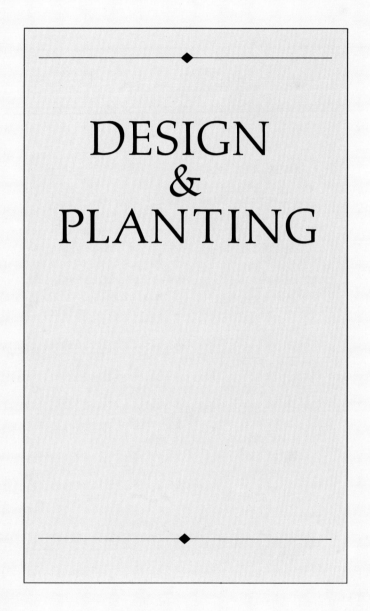

DESIGN
&
PLANTING

A Sense of Place

JOHN BROOKES

Fontwell lies at the foot of the South Downs, five miles from the sea, and it is there that the present owner of Denmans, Mrs Robinson, began to develop a highly original garden, about three and a half acres in extent, in 1946. Its most striking feature is the way in which many choice plants are allowed to self-seed and ramble in ground liberally mulched with gravel.

My first visit was just before Christmas, to many gardeners the low point of the year. In my mind's eye, however, I could easily imagine the walled garden bursting with perennials, herbs and old-fashioned roses and the architectural masses of the plants growing on a hot south-facing terrace.

Since 1980, John Brookes has run the garden and his School of Landscape and Garden Design from Clock House, formerly a stable block within Denmans Garden. His courses – well-known and respected in the USA and Europe as well as in Britain – and his numerous books have had a major influence on many gardeners, opening the doors to a less insular and more open approach to the best in other traditions. The idea that a garden should be treated as a living space as well as providing space for plants is increasingly relevant in the highly urbanized world of today, where gardens are steadily getting smaller.

A strictly horticultural approach to gardens is less and less appropriate to the small plots of land attached to modern houses. It is increasingly common to judge a garden successful when the design takes into account the lifestyles of the people who are going to use it. This generous paved area close to a house is useful for sitting out and is brightened by plants that tolerate dry conditions.

I GOT MY FIRST TASTE of designing during my apprenticeship at the Nottingham Parks Department. I knew at once that this was what I wanted to do and ever since have been very lucky to be able to work in a discipline that gives me so much pleasure. I am sure that many people think that designing is all imagination and fine feeling, a matter of selecting with taste from the vast range of plants available, paying careful attention to the way colours harmonize and contrast with one another and to the pattern of seasonal change. That is not my kind of designing; plants are not the only or, for that matter, the first thing that

I think about. I want to create a garden that suits the needs of the people who are going to use it. Before I start planning on paper I like to hear from them. Clients who want to off-load on the designer the job of working out their priorities make me angry. To simply say, 'You know best', leaves me without the essential information for working out a design scheme.

Designing the modern garden

The modern garden has to take account of our present-day lifestyle. The gardens of the past are, of course, rich in ideas for us. But whatever we take from them has to be interpreted in terms of the way we live now. An important factor is the amount of time available for looking after a garden. Herbaceous borders in the style of Gertrude Jekyll, with wonderfully subtle combinations of colour and texture, might be very attractive but to bring them to perfection as she did at Munstead Wood requires an army of gardeners. Our gardens are shrinking and so is the amount of time we have available to look after them; there are many leisure alternatives to pruning roses and digging potatoes.

Partly because of changes in lifestyle, partly because gardens are smaller now, they are required to satisfy many functions, of which the display of plants is only one. And what we want of a garden does not remain constant throughout our lives. For young people without children the need may be for an open-air area that can be used for relaxing and entertaining. For a family with small children the priority will probably be the provision of play areas that can be easily supervised. As the children get a bit older a larger area might be devoted to growing vegetables and when they have grown up there may be more time and inclination for growing ornamental plants. A point is reached, however, when management becomes a burden if the planting and the layout is not simplified. Throughout all the phases in an owner's life the garden can serve as an extension of the house and the more relaxed the feeling it creates the better. We have to get out of our minds the notion that horticultural excellence is the only standard by which a garden should be judged if we are going to make the most of our small spaces.

Practical considerations
The very ordinary day-to-day aspects of our lifestyle need to be taken into account right at the beginning. Perhaps there has to be room for car parking or you may want to erect a garage in a position with easy access to the house, but not so that it occupies the best part of the garden. A space has to be found to store rubbish where it is easily reached but out of the way and perhaps the same applies to an area for drying clothes. Most gardens need a space for storing tools and equipment, and garden furniture that must be put away during the winter months. There are other practical features that you may have to include, too, from an oil storage tank to a compost heap. If the service features of a garden are not thought out right at the beginning, it is very difficult to fit them in at a later stage. Their location will determine where you need to lay some of your hard surfaces.

Aesthetic factors

Finding a way of satisfying the needs of those who are going to use it is the first step in designing a successful garden but there are other general points to consider, too. It is important, for instance, that it should be appropriate to its physical setting. In towns the landscape is so cluttered by buildings that the natural environment doesn't have to be taken into account to the same extent so that there is the opportunity for a theatricality that in the country would be quite out of place. Equally, a country garden, loosely structured and cottagey, strikes a false note in a setting that is dominated by urban bricks, stone and concrete. The natural landscape should be taken into account in your equation. If you can use local materials – and you can get a good idea of what they are by looking at older buildings and gardens in the area – so much the better. To get them you may have to go to some trouble; garden-centre merchandizing of plants, materials and equipments is encouraging uniformity and standardization. If you can't get local materials new, it is worth trying to obtain them secondhand.

If the house is already a mature element in the landscape, the design of the garden and the materials used must be in sympathy with it. Textured concrete paving slabs may go very well with the bold lines and fabric of a modern house but, if they are not used carefully, might clash horribly laid close to walls of mellow brick. In many gardens it is this transitional area, close to the house, that requires the most careful treatment: matching materials – brick to brick, for instance – or at least using materials that combine happily.

Establishing a link between the inside and the outside of the house is something that has been learned from countries with warm climates

The transitional area where house interior and garden meet is particularly important when the aim of the design is to promote a relaxed style of living. Plants play a secondary role around a sunny paved area where there is room for taking meals outdoors.

but it is just as valid in the cool, moist climate of Britain as elsewhere. A floodlit, snowy garden in winter seen from a warm interior is an important visual extension of the house, although not as practical as a sunny terrace for eating out in summer. The link can be strengthened by the use of decorative or structural elements that cross the threshold. My own dining-room at the Clock House opens on to a paved terrace with overhead beams that are stained to match the wood of the doors. The use of plants in containers inside and outside also helps to bridge the divide so that one area merges into the other.

If the house is mature, some sort of garden is likely to exist already but it should be viewed in the same critical way as a new piece of ground. Does the garden as it exists meet your requirements? If not, are there features of it that could be incorporated in a scheme more suited to your needs? Is it worth reconsidering your first ideas in the light of outstanding existing features, such as a good stone or brick wall? As in all aspects of the preliminary stages of designing, you must take time to get a feel of what is there and to appreciate how best it can be used. But once you have made your decision and are clear about what you want, you may have to be ruthless. One is naturally reluctant to remove trees and shrubs but, if they are badly positioned and cannot be moved, they may have to be cut down.

Making a plan

Whatever the size of the garden, do get a plan on paper before making any changes on the site. The easiest way is to begin with a rough sketch of the area on which you can record the measurements as you take them. You can then transfer these measurements to a plan drawn to scale – preferably one to fifty for a small garden, although for something larger it may need to be one to a hundred. Mark on the plan the scale and the various points of the compass, for you will need to bear the sun's direction in mind when laying out your garden. Make sure that windows, doors and all existing features are recorded, and it helps to include those outside the garden's periphery that are significant; for example, because they cast shade. Once you have got an accurate record on paper you can begin to be more specific about allocating areas. If you use gridded paper, it will be much easier to get an accurate idea of the proportions and pattern of your design.

Priorities

There are a few general points to consider as you make your plan. The distribution of sun and shade is always important in the garden, one of the difficulties being that there are a lot of elements competing for a position in the sun. Few vegetables will succeed in a shaded area and under trees the competition for nutrients and water will also restrict the range of plants that can be grown. Ornamental pools, swimming pools and greenhouses all need open positions, while terraces and swimming pools need shelter that may have to be added in the form of hedges and fences.

Privacy is another factor to be taken into account, although it is not worth getting obsessive about this if, to achieve it, other aspects of the garden are going to suffer. A mistake that many gardeners make is to work from the boundaries in rather than from the house outwards so that the garden becomes a curiously isolated pocket and outside features that could add to its interest and beauty are lost. At the Clock House, the former stable block of Denmans where I now run courses in garden design, the .2 ha (½-acre) garden flows into the 1.2 ha (three-acre) garden created over the last thirty years by Mrs Joyce Robinson. The only boundary between the two gardens is a drive.

All or part of the garden may be suited to a symmetrical, formal arrangement, as might be the case if it is attached to a period house of symmetrical architecture. However, a less formal design allows for a more flexible treatment of the various units that go to make up the garden and can help to create a more relaxing environment. But even when there is no symmetry, there must be a sense of balance and proportion. Without it a garden will be an agitating assembly of parts that does not make a coherent whole. A small garden, in particular, is like a piece of sculpture, where there has to be a balanced proportion of bulky masses and voids.

Plants are the main constituents of the garden that transform a two-dimensional scheme into something in three dimensions. But putting them in should be delayed until as much of the main structural work can be done as finances will allow. If construction work is to be done in phases, it is important to work out the implications of delaying major jobs, such as changing levels within the garden or installing features such as pools.

Although steps can be a practical inconvenience (making for difficulties with wheelbarrows and other wheeled traffic), or even a hazard if not well built and equipped with a handrail, small changes of level in a garden can be a great advantage, introducing an element of drama that can be accentuated by the materials used in the construction and by skilful planting. Making a garden on several levels, however, does call for extra care at the planning stage.

Water attracts attention very strongly. Its reflecting surface and its sound and movement can add enormously to the quality of a garden and its installation has now been made relatively easy with the availability of flexible liners and pre-formed rigid shapes. However, informal pools rarely look satisfactory close to buildings, as they would be in small gardens, and the irregular pre-formed shapes can even look absurd. Pools, like railway sleepers (as used in paving and for making raised beds) are in danger of becoming gardening clichés. Fashions in gardening, as in everything else, are so powerful that it is sometimes difficult to see how trapped one is in following a trend.

Plants and planting

Planting, as I have said, introduces the third dimension to the garden and for that reason alone is important. But I must stress that making a fascinating collection of plants and growing them to perfection is only one kind of gardening. It is very satisfying for those who enjoy it but there are many who, while wanting an agreeable outdoor room, are not especially interested in the vast range of cultivated plants available and who want reliable and attractive performers rather than the species and varieties that excite the plantsman or plantswoman.

Even when working with a small range of plants, there are some keys to success. The first is to know your soil: how dry or moist it is and how acid or alkaline (this last point is easily established using a simple soil-testing kit). Many plants will tolerate a wide range of conditions but most of the acid-loving plants, especially rhododendrons, will not thrive in lime. The local climate and the micro-climate conditions of your garden will also affect the plants you can grow. Although there are many that are extremely hardy even in the worst conditions Britain can throw at them, others are tender to varying degrees and some are particularly vulnerable to sudden frosts.

The durable beauty of foliage can be much more useful in the garden than short-lived floral displays and is especially important from late autumn until mid-spring. Contrasts of texture and leaf shape add greatly to the interest of a garden.

Successful planting begins by being aware of the conditions your garden offers and matching plants to them. But a good result can never be achieved by picking one of this and one of that in a well-meant but whimsical fashion. Something of this effect can even be seen in some of the great plant collections, where the overall impression is of an extraordinary muddled assembly of leaves and flowers.

Bear in mind that flowers are often very transitory while leaves last for months on end, in the case of evergreens for all twelve months of the year. The colour of flowers when they are in bloom can be subtly beautiful or brilliantly exciting but a sustained display of harmonizing or complementary shades calls for enthusiastic management. Foliage, too, far from being uniformly green, is wonderfully varied in colour, texture, shape and size. Most of us are glad to have some colour in the garden but it is a sad mistake to think that a garden in which flowers are not the dominant element is essentially inferior. This is not the case, as many gardeners of today and yesterday have shown.

When using colour, bear in mind that certain moods are associated with some ranges. Soft blues and pinks, for example, create a restful atmosphere when used with purple and white, whereas yellows and oranges have a liveliness that makes them more appropriate in some settings than in others.

The planting that underlies the decorative interest of flower colour gives a framework to the garden. For this you need plants that give bulk, some of which should be evergreen to carry the garden through the winter. But you also need a few star performers (not too many) strategically placed to provide focal points in the garden. For this you might use a tree of striking leaf shape (and vivid autumn colouring) such as *Rhus typhina*, or spiky plants, such as the yuccas.

Many factors are going to be involved in your choice but it does help to be aware of the period in which a plant was introduced to a particular kind of garden. The monkey puzzle tree (*Araucaria auracana*), for example, is a classic feature of Victorian villa gardens while the cedar of Lebanon (*Cedrus libani*) is firmly associated with eighteenth-century landscape gardens. There is something inappropriate about planting either in the other's territory. There is a rightness about trees in other positions, too. For example, birches (species of *Betula*) look fine in country settings but uncomfortable in the cramped conditions of a town, whereas many of the showier, cultivated trees shriek discomfort when planted in a natural setting.

Your planting scheme also has to take into account the growth rate of plants. Trees may take many years to reach maturity but even shrubs will take three or four years to fill out; in the meantime you might consider using short-lived plants – annuals, biennials or perennials – to give bulk to the planting in the first few years.

The life-cycle of plants ensures that the garden is never static. However, despite our national reputation as gardeners, we sometimes behave as though nothing ever changes. We humans have our own life-cyle, too, and our gardens should reflect that what we need of them is not fixed in one ultimate scheme. We should be more open to influences from other countries and more ready to see that our requirements change.

The Formal Element

◆
─────────────────────────────────────

CHRISTOPHER MASSON

Several years ago, a friend introduced me to a young New Zealander who had come to England in 1975 to pursue a career in garden design after training in fine arts and industrial design in his native country. On seeing Christopher Masson's own garden and following a visit to Sissinghurst with him, I was immediately impressed by his knowledge of English gardens and the uncluttered enthusiasm for plants and gardens that allowed him to see them with fresh eyes. What struck me particularly about his own small garden, now in other hands, was the way a simple formal structure, modest though the scale was, could hold together a rich collection of interesting plants. It was a model of the way a small London garden can be transformed into something individual and special, without falling into the trap of grotesque overstatement.

As a visit to the Chelsea Flower Show makes depressingly clear, overstatement is the language of many professional designers. To them, every garden seems to be a potential 'garden centre'. Christopher Masson is himself generous in acknowledging that in Britain there are many highly gifted and knowledgeable amateur gardeners from whom professionals have much to learn. Perhaps talented amateurs will be as important as professionals in the revival of formal gardening.

─────────────────────────────────────
◆

Hidcote Manor in Gloucestershire is one of the most exciting gardens created in England this century. Its maker, Major Lawrence Johnston, imposed a formal structure of hedged enclosures on an unpromising and exposed site. There is much to be learnt at Hidcote about luxuriant planting within a framework of living architecture.

IT IS EASY TO FALL INTO THE HABIT of thinking that everything to do with the garden, plants and garden design included, is untouched by fashion. This is not the case, however; fashion in the garden may not change at the hectic pace it does in the home but change it certainly does. Thirty years ago who would have expected to find a modern suburban gardener stripping the turf from his lawn, carting away the topsoil and sowing a mixture of meadow-grass and wild-flower seed. The conservation garden, not surprisingly given how extreme some of

the measures advocated can be, is not the only current fashion. In the 1950s who would have expected that the willow-leaved pear (*Pyrus salicifolia*) would become a cliché of small gardens (though always a beautiful one) and that hostas, epimediums and true geraniums would be common border plants? We live in a period with an exceptional range of competing fashions in gardening, each with its own ranking of desirable plants, colours and arrangements, the exponents of some making rather harsh judgements on whatever does not conform to their own canons of good taste.

It is perfectly natural that we should be influenced by current trends and fashions. But the gardeners one most admires are those discriminating and independent spirits who create something so marked by their own originality that it transcends all fashions. It is a great strength of British gardening that it continues to produce so many talented amateurs as well as professionals. In the course of my work I often have the opportunity to appreciate the judgement and flair of twentieth-century designers such as Peter Coates, Geoffrey Jellicoe and Lanning Roper. It doesn't detract from my admiration for them to say that one of the best small gardens I know is right next door to me in a south London suburb. It is the work of amateurs who are knowledgeable about plants and who have shown great imagination in making the most of a relatively small space. Nothing looks as though it has been bought off the peg at the garden centre; everything bears the stamp of their own discerning judgment and experience.

Formal Revival

One trend in design that can be detected in the gardens of both amateurs and professionals is a return to formality. The miniaturized landscape, with its sinuous lines and irregular 'natural' shapes, is giving way to gardens arranged on a stricter grid or radiating pattern, with clearly defined main axes linking the principal buildings on the site to focal points, visual incidents created or exploited by the gardener. The formal garden shows its bones, frankly acknowledging that it is a controlled environment and making a virtue of sharply defined shapes and areas, and of symmetrical arrangement. Although it can be rich in historical associations, even to the point of being planted with the strict severity of seventeenth-century models, once the structure has been established the planting within a formal layout is a matter of taste.

Two of the great gardens of the twentieth century, Hidcote Manor in Gloucestershire and Sissinghurst Castle in Kent, demonstrate how gardens of essentially formal structure can take exuberant planting. In both gardens there are grand effects, but the formality is not expressed in intimidating grand schemes. The character of both is very intimate, the small interconnecting compartments of which they are composed so richly planted that throughout much of the year the visitor is more conscious of what is contained than of the enclosures.

The formal trend is one that I think even more gardeners ought to consider. Its advantages are obvious for a garden that is surrounded by or in close proximity to buildings. Its axes and focal points can be related to doors and windows, making a coherent ensemble of architecture and garden. This is as true with a large garden as it is with a small one, although, if you have got the good fortune to be working on a generous scale, there is scope for allowing the formal part of the garden to merge with an area that is less structured. However, perhaps the greatest advantage of a formal arrangement is that the structure of the garden will be interesting in its own right throughout all four seasons; plants may come and go but the skeleton of the garden will remain even in the depths of winter. And the better the materials you use for such elements as hedges, walls and paving the finer the effect will be.

Another advantage of a formal layout is that, if combined with a planting of low-maintenance shrubs and perennials, it makes one of the best solutions for a garden that will have to endure periods of neglect. It may never produce the moments of high exhilaration that you might get in a plantsman's garden but it can give a respectable year-round performance.

I know, however, from personal experience how difficult it can be to persuade clients that what they want (delphiniums and hollyhocks) is not compatible with the conditions in their garden (shaded town rectangles overhung by dripping lime trees) or with the time they have available for maintenance. While I am in this plangent mood, let me say how galling it is to do a planting scheme in agreement with a client, who then interplants to fill the temporary gaps and allows the interplanting to take over – then expresses surprise that the original scheme has not come to fruition. How fortunate the person who gardens on his or her own account and remains untroubled by such irritations.

Initial Planning

Whether you already have an established garden or you are starting from scratch, for a formal layout, decide early where you want your main axes and vistas and how you want to divide the area between pedestrian and planting zones. You will certainly need a ground-plan drawn to scale. I find, however, that before I note things on it, I need to make many quick sketches of what I have in front of me and of the

One of the first decisions to make when planning a garden is the direction of main axes and vistas. The ornaments or features that close a vista can be added at a much later stage. This flagstoned path, flanked by roses, is at Tintinhull House, Somerset.

various ways that I could modify it. Some people will find it useful to take photographs, building up a portfolio of views, not only looking away from the house but also looking back at it. Having a dated record of the stages in a garden's development is highly instructive and very encouraging.

Paving

A generous paved area near the house is an invaluable asset and one that needs to be tied in to your vistas and axes. In a country so famed for its lawns the pressure to include one is sometimes overwhelming. Unfortunately the ideal we see in our mind's eye, inspired by magnificent examples such as the Theatre Lawn at Hidcote Manor, is not easily realized in a town garden. I have steadily moved to being very anti-lawn for the small garden. There is generally too much traffic concentrated on a relatively small area but, even when there are hard surfaces that allow you to get from point A to point B, the turf will deteriorate because of poor light and lack of air movement. I am sure that this last point, one that is not often taken account of, contributes to many of the problems of growing plants in small town gardens that are closed in by buildings and walls.

When choosing your paving materials, I strongly recommend getting the best quality your budget will allow. Regrettably, York stone has become prohibitively expensive for most people. It is such a subtle material, creating a pleasingly uniform look but with just enough colour and textural variation so that it is never bland. If I am free to use natural materials for a small area my first choice would probably be granite setts. They are much more varied in colour than York stone, pinks, greens and shades of grey showing up particularly well when they are wet. Their sheen and pock-marks add to their interest. I have found that on clay soils particularly, where the ground is moving all the time, they move well, adjusting to the shifting contours. Cobbles are very attractive visually but they are too uncomfortable to walk on to merit being used over an extended area. They are useful as contrast to other materials or as an incident to mark a change of direction. Tiles laid on edge, which used to be positioned round features such as well-heads, are also useful effective marking an accent in a path.

I use brick a great deal. Old brick paths with a subdued pattern just showing through can be really lovely but brick can sometimes look rather busy. I am about to do a garden where the clients have asked for an area to be laid in white bricks, which will need very good pointing with silver sand and white cement. I have yet to be totally convinced that this is a good idea. In a bright light the paving might seem too startling and there is also the chance of unsightly staining, particularly where there is drip from overhead trees. However I may well be won over because this paving will be used in conjunction with clipped box and other hedging.

The general advice always to use frost-resistant bricks is not something about which I feel obsessive. Clearly you can't risk using bricks that might shatter where there are steps and you probably need simple clean surfaces near buildings and main access points. But, provided that you have got the time for maintenance, it can be very

The choice of materials used for hard surfaces and the manner in which they are laid can make or mar a garden. This handsome pattern is made of granite setts laid in gravel. Gravel is a very versatile material that combines well with other surfaces.

attractive to have a hard surface with moss and other small plants coming through it to add a sense of relief.

Reconstituted stone and man-made materials are competitive in price – and some are very good – but I like to mix them with other materials in a setting where there is strong planting. In a large expanse they can be rather bland in appearance; they would be much better if their surfaces were pitted and irregular.

Unless you are using it as a security measure – it is difficult to walk quietly over gravel or pea shingle – loose surfaces are not practical near a house. You need a transitional surface so that you do not bring small stones indoors on the soles of your shoes. But gravel is a material that I do like to use very much. It combines well with other materials, something that can be exploited decoratively; for example, a square of York stone or nicely patterned brick can make an attractive incident at a point where two gravel paths meet. I have also used gravel in a less formal way to give unity to a garden scheme, raking it through under trees and shrubs, more or less as a mulch, even planting perennials in it. There is certainly scope for more widespread use of it along these lines.

Boundaries and divisions

It is often said that the true test of a garden is to see it in winter. I wonder if other gardeners get as much pleasure as I do from the off-season clear-out, when everything that is dead and untidy is got rid off. Once all the rubbish has gone, you see the walls and hedges, the defining boundaries and internal divisions of the garden for what they are. It is the moment when quality counts. Unfortunately, to get quality you have either got to spend money to have walls built or you have to allow time for good hedges to grow. I hope that the present tendency for home-owners to move house quite frequently won't encourage the use of showy short-term effects at the expense of quality.

Living boundaries and dividers are some of the loveliest features that a garden can have. One has to be quite realistic, however, and recognize that to trim a hedge is time-consuming, even though with the best materials, such as yew, it needs to be done only once a year. When clients cannot guarantee the level of maintenance that hedges need I recommend constructed formality.

Box (*Buxus sempervirens*) and yew (*Taxus baccata*) may seem very obvious as hedging materials but their virtues are such that there are few if any plants to match them. Yew is superb for taller hedging; it can be trimmed to very sharp, clean lines and its dense texture provides a marvellous background for plants or ornaments and makes an excellent contrast to stone and brickwork. Some find its dark green too lugubrious but to many the sombre solidity of a plain yew hedge is infinitely preferable to the yellow-green of some of its cultivars, even in the depths of winter.

Box, like yew, is suitable for sun or shade but it grows too slowly for tall hedges. It is, in fact, the classic plant of traditional formal gardens, used as an edging and to form the geometric patterns of the old knot gardens, and, in its dwarf form (*B. s.* 'Suffruticosa'), elaborately planted in scrolls and arabesques in the magnificent *parterre de broderie* that were first developed in French gardens during the sixteenth century. Box, which responds well to clipping, has never lost its popularity as an edging plant, although often, as at Cranborne in Dorset, its historical associations play a part in its choice.

The baroque curves of a *parterre de broderie* are not for the small garden but with the current trend to formality we are likely to see many more box-edged borders and perhaps a revived interest in the knot garden. A small knot garden of box and lavender at Mottisfont Abbey in Hampshire, where the National Trust maintains the national collection of old roses, gives a very good idea of the way such a feature could be adapted to a modern garden. The designer, Norah Lindsay, was inspired by old patterns for knots but there is no reason why the modern gardener shouldn't adopt a more adventurous approach. It is worth mentioning in passing that the old authorities on gardening made a distinction between open and closed knots. In the former the area enclosed by the pattern was bare, although very often made more decorative by the use of coloured earths, such as crushed brick. In the latter the area enclosed by the pattern was planted out with flowers, generally of one kind to produce a massed effect.

Although box was the most long-lasting of the edging plants used by the Elizabethan and Stuart gardeners it was far from being the only one. Aromatic and scented plants such as lavender, rosemary and santolina were particularly popular and are still very useful for sunny gardens. Remember, though, that they do need quite a lot of attention. They must be cut back really hard if they are to be long-lived and they are inclined to die back if other plants grow too close to them,

Deciduous hedges, for instance of beech (*Fagus sylvatica*) or hornbeam (*Carpinus betulus*), have a distinctive beauty in winter and early spring as well as making leafy divisions in summer. This hedge at Cranborne Manor separates a formal section of the garden from an area of meadow.

competing for light, moisture and nutrients.

To return briefly to the larger hedging plants, a word has to be said in favour of holly (*Ilex aquifolium*), although it is very slow growing and it can be difficult to work among. If it is neglected and you have to weed out and clean round the base it can be a nightmare but it is a hedge I am always pleased to see in someone else's garden. I have several times seen it used very successfully as a constituent of a tapestry hedge, that is a hedge composed of more than one kind of plant. It goes well with privet (*Ligustrum ovalifolium*), though their different rates of growth mean that you need to take particular care over clipping.

Two deciduous hedging plants that are beautiful in their own rights, and attractive to use in conjunction with evergreens, are beech (*Fagus sylvatica*) and hornbeam (*Carpinus betulus*). In autumn the leaves turn russet but do not fall so that they create lovely warm splashes of colour when lit by wintry sun. The ambitious gardener might try pleaching hornbeams, or other broadleaved trees such as limes (*Tilia*). Pleaching is a system of training branches horizontally in a single plane, resulting in what is sometimes described as a hedge on stilts. The best-known example is at Hidcote Manor and it is such a tour de force that one can imagine it inspiring committed gardeners to try it in a scaled-down version.

Close trimming is a highly finished kind of formality but the mere lining out of plants is in itself an ordered arrangement. And there are lots of plants that, although not suitable for the close shaping that yew or box, for example, will take, can be used as informal hedges (a term that rather understates the order that these hedges impose on a site).

Shrubs that flower over a long season, such as the recurrent roses, are very useful. In my own planting I favour the rugosas, which are easy and reliable, good in leaf and flower, and in some cases, for instance 'Frau Dagmar Hastrup', completing their performance by producing a handsome display of hips. The very vigorous floribunda

'Queen Elizabeth' is an example of a rose that, because of its vertical gaunt habit, is best used planted out in lines, with geraniums or something similar growing at the base to mask the bare stems. But roses are just a starting point; the imaginative gardener has great scope for choosing informal hedging plants not only on the grounds of flowering performance but also on account of their foliage and habit.

Symmetrical arrangements
As the geometry of knot gardens and parterres demonstrates, it is mainly through the symmetrical arrangements of parts within the garden that its formality is sustained. This can sometimes be at a very discreet level. For instance, an apparently informal planting either side of a path can have an underlying rhythm that subtly creates a symmetrical pattern. This is sometimes achieved with plants of such loose growth – for example, lady's mantle (*Alchemilla mollis*) or catmint (*Nepeta* 'Six Hills Giant') – that the eye responds to the symmetry without analysing how it has been achieved.

More often, however, the symmetry is an emphatic statement that is intended to be read as such. You find it on a grand scale in the splendid avenues of trees that are such a lovely feature of many country houses. However, the scale need not be grand. At Tintinhull House, a National Trust property in Somerset, the central path is flanked by paired bushes of clipped box, giving a calm, measured pace to the garden.

In a small garden there may not be the scope for an extended symmetrical arrangement. But even a foursome of plants arranged at the corners of a paved area or a pair flanking a gateway or a short flight of steps will be enough to create a symmetrical accent. For the symmetry to be really impressive plants need to be well matched in size and shape and, therefore, the plants that are favoured for these effects either respond well to training or are of naturally controlled shape. We can expect to see a great revival in the use of clipped balls and cones of box – the continental suppliers are going to be very busy – for they are very versatile and stand up to shady conditions very much better than most other plants.

There are, however, other plants that are worth considering. Bay (*Laurus nobilis*), for example, can be treated in a variety of ways, most commonly either as a pyramid or as a ball on a standard. You sometimes see it surviving in the most awful conditions but it can succumb in harsh winters like those that we have had over the last few years. Clipping seems to make it vulnerable to a pest or disease that causes the leaves to curl so I am trying a regime of clipping in late spring and spraying straight after. I hope that this will get round the problem.

There are handsome flowering plants available, too, that work well in symmetrical arrangements. The ready availability of standard marguerites (*Chrysanthemum frutescens*) is a clear sign of the revived interest in formal gardens. Perhaps we can expect their price to come down as production increases to meet demand. A plant that I hope we will see a lot more of is *Anisodonthera capensis*. It has been available in the last few years as a standard and seems to be marginally hardier than the marguerite, although it needs the protection of a cold greenhouse during the worst weather. It has a pretty little leaf and a bluish flower rather like a miniature hibiscus. One of its great virtues is that it has a long flowering season.

Foliage plants We can expect other plants, too, to become more readily available as trained specimens. Already the bushy little willow *Salix helvetica* is fairly widely stocked as a standard; it makes a tight, grey, rounded head. I have also recently come across *Caragana arborescens* grown on a single stem. It has an attractive pattern of feathery leaves and in May has pale yellow flowers. It does not cut out much light and other plants can be grown right underneath it.

Rather than searching out the unfamiliar, however, it can be worth trying to look with fresh eyes at plants that have become part of the standard repertoire. The willow leaved pear, for example, is used time and time again as a focal point, to close a vista at the end of a path. It will always be a very good plant but how refreshing to see it used in another way, perhaps one at each corner of a sunken garden. Familiarity has also dulled our appreciation of *Robinia pseudoacacia* 'Frisia'; perhaps we would re-evaluate it if we saw it used in a fresh way.

Trained plants

Even when they are not forming part of a symmetrical arrangement, shaped plants give a distinctly formal tone to a garden. There are unlikely to be gardeners now who could contemplate creating a solemn assembly of topiary on the scale of that at Packwood House in Warwickshire or a quaint collection as fantastic as that at Levens Hall in Cumbria but the topiary tradition is still alive in cottage as well as in grand gardens. Yew and box remain the classic plants for such precise training but plants such as holly and Portugal laurel (*Prunus lusitanica*) can be used for more general shapes.

I am particularly fond of Portugal laurel and have had some success shaping this plant. In one case I have reduced an amorphous shape to a drum and I have planted another Portugal laurel that I am planning to train into a matching 'drum'. In another garden where an untidy bush of Portugal laurel was blocking a view from a dining-room window I clipped the base into a square, cleaned out the middle and mushroomed the top. I am not sure how far one can take this rather free approach to topiary but I am applying it also to a lump of yew that was sitting rather clumsily in the middle of a lawn. Having clipped it into a bell shape, I am leaving the top to grow loosely until it dictates its own shape.

Trained fruit trees also set a formal tone in a garden. Mature fans, cordons and espaliers are highly decorative as well as productive and can be accommodated in quite a confined space. The growing of trained fruit trees is, however, not something to undertake lightly. It is not that the skills required are so specialized that they would defeat the ordinary gardener but building up the framework and the subsequent maintenance call for long-term commitment. If you are prepared to give it, they make very worthwhile additions to the garden.

Other Formal Garden Features

These features can powerfully reinforce the formality of a garden's layout. It is important that they are in the right scale if they are to hold

One of the simplest ways to establish a formal tone within a garden is to arrange elements within it symmetrically. Containers of matching plants, which can be moved about and changed according to season, are a useful supplement to more permanent features.

the eye at the end of a vista, mark a change of direction in a path, or flank a doorway symmetrically. Sometimes masses of little pots can look wonderful but to make a clear statement they need to be skilfully grouped. The formal solution to the placing of these elements is often the easiest. It takes discrimination and a very sure eye to find an informal arrangement that works. Particularly when the garden is on a small scale, an unsuccessful informal arrangement can be very distracting, an eyecatcher of the worst kind.

Ornaments

In the case of ornaments, more often than not it is a matter of finding a place that needs something, leaving it empty until the right thing comes along or making do with a simple terracotta pot in the short term. Sometimes it is reassuring to discover that all you needed was a well-planted pot and not a Michelangelo after all. Some reproduction ornaments are truly awful but I am not opposed to using reproductions on principle; there is a very long tradition of using good, reproduction statuary in gardens.

Unless ornaments are set on a base, they very often look as though they are going to walk away or that they shouldn't really be where they are. They need to be raised on a small pedestal in order to look as though they belong. Pots, too, are greatly improved if they are set on a base. I like to have permanent pedestals in strategic positions where I can ring the changes from time to time.

Garden architecture

There is not the same flexibility with garden buildings or even some of the heavier garden furniture. When I speak of garden buildings I am not talking of the tool shed at the bottom of the garden but of something conceived as an ornamental feature in the garden.

Conservatories, gazebos and other forms of garden architecture are coming back into fashion, and manufacturers are working hard to meet the demand. I have found that the use of garden architecture need not be limited to gardens on a grand scale. For instance, I have used a small hexagonal gazebo with trellis-work sides in a London garden of very modest size and it has made an elegant focal point.

Pergolas, too, are coming back into fashion, although not built on the monumental scale that the Edwardians favoured. As I found in a recent project, it is quite possible to accommodate a pergola in a town garden of medium size. In my view, it is a mistake to aim for the heavily shaded effect that is so desirable in a Mediterranean setting. You can, of course, afford to have a dark shaded covered area if your garden is so large that there are plenty of others that are open and sunny. But in a country where the sun has enough trouble to struggle feebly through cloud cover you want an airy sheltered walkway with dappled light, not a dank slippery tunnel. To get the desired effect I have kept the number of cross-beams to a minimum; at the moment it still looks rather raw and bare but in a year or two it will be clothed in climbers, making a handsome structure aligned with the main door leading on to the garden. The closer a pergola is to a building the more architectural it needs to be. But a pergola that is at a distance can be very simple, even rather crudely executed. It needs to relate to other elements in the garden's layout but what is important is that it allows you to lift plants to a decent height.

Water

Water can be a very lovely addition to a garden. Reflections give the garden another dimension and, if you have a small jet installed, you have the pleasure of the sight and sound of moving water. The installation of pools has become much easier. You can choose between rigid pre-moulded shapes or flexible liners, which can be installed by anyone who is reasonably handy, (electric recycling pumps, which are quite inexpensive to run, make a jet a delightful addition).

On the whole, the formal garden needs a formal shape, a square, circle, hexagon, or the like, but in a garden of reasonable size you might use water to mark a transition to an area that is less formally planted and then a gently irregular shape might be appropriate. I have used this device in a reasonably large London garden, where a bank behind the pool is informally planted, the planting looking as though it is coming forward, the water as though it is running back so that you don't see where one begins and ends. In my own garden, which is smaller, water has been treated in a more severe way, with a formal channel running across almost the full width.

Importance of Visual Appeal

Perhaps I have left the impression that I am preoccupied with the formal arrangement of various garden elements. If I have, the impression is misleading. I see that there can be great advantages in terms of management in the formal arrangement of a garden and I respond to the visual appeal of a garden where I can see the structure showing through. As a designer I enjoy using the elements touched on here and others, too. I have made no mention, for instance, of the way that trelliswork can be used. All that said, the gardens that give me the greatest pleasure are those that show the hand of a knowledgeable and enthusiastic plantsman or plantswoman, where the formality contains a profusion of plants imaginatively combined to make the most of texture and colour.

To the designer it is sometimes a source of frustration that there is never a single solution to the problems he or she is trying to resolve. Ultimately, however, that is what helps to make gardens such an unfailing source of delight.

Every Plant in its Place

BETH CHATTO

For many visitors to the Chelsea Flower Show, the quiet beauty of Beth Chatto's stand makes a deliciously refreshing pause in what can sometimes seem an almost exhausting blaze of colour. Colour, of course, is not excluded from her displays, but flowers in them are less important *per se* than the associations she makes between plants requiring similar growing conditions. In these, foliage texture, shape and colour are just as important as flowers.

A living demonstration of just how effective these associations can be, is the garden at White Barn House in Essex that Beth Chatto and her husband have created over the years, starting in the early 1960s. Here is an achievement that will reinvigorate the enthusiasm of those faced with the problems of a difficult site. Until the Chattos set to work, the garden here was a gravelly wasteland interrupted by a soggy hollow; now it is a mature garden containing an outstanding collection of plants – perennials in particular – grouped with a rare sensitivity to qualities of foliage and shape as well as to colour. Beside the garden is Beth Chatto's nursery, which has established an enviable reputation for providing good stock of an exciting range of unusual plants.

It is difficult to imagine how Mrs Chatto has found time to write about her garden. When I visited her, on a day when the very early daffodil 'Cedric Morris' was brightening the garden, she was at work on her latest book, a notebook of the rich experience – human and gardening – that is part of the yearly cycle in the life of this very busy and gifted plantswoman.

SO MUCH OF GARDENING is a matter of common sense but when you are starting out, it is not always easy to know what is common sense in relation to plants. This is as true of plant associations as it is of other aspects of gardening.

My own experience of making a garden – and subsequently a nursery – from a neglected piece of East Anglian farmland may hold lessons for

other gardeners. The scale on which I now garden can give a misleading impression. I did not set out to build up a successful business or to make a garden that would be visited by the public. My ambition was simply to make a garden that pleased me. To do that I had to come to terms with the soils and growing conditions of my site, and to find plant associations appropriate to them in the same way as any gardener must who wants to make the most of the raw materials available.

In the garden that Beth Chatto and her husband have created at White Barn Farm in Essex, many of the finest associations are of plants with contrasting textures and patterns of foliage and subtle combinations of leaf colour. Flowers are a bonus.

Plants of Distinction

Although I had much to learn, I wasn't an absolute beginner when I started the garden at White Barn Farm. My husband and I had had seventeen years' experience of gardening on boulder clay several miles away and I had already learnt the value of drought-tolerant plants. We wanted to make a garden on this particular site because we felt there was the opportunity here to grow a tremendous range of plants and to make a series of gardens, each with a different character.

We were not thinking in terms of rose gardens and herbaceous borders full of cultivars, such as 'improved' delphiniums, Michaelmas daisies, phloxes and pyrethrums. Quite early in my gardening I had realized that, although I loved flowers, they were to me a bonus. What I wanted in my garden above all else was the pattern of leaves, so that I could enjoy their shapes and the contrasts of form, texture and scale that they create. Right from the beginning I had grown what to some were unusual plants, species plants rather than cultivars. The balanced character of the species, often with interesting foliage that lasts for months, sometimes the whole year, enhanced perhaps for a short season by flowers, has remained infinitely more appealing to me than the highly coloured creations of the plant breeders.

Natural groupings

My attitude to plants and to gardens has been very much influenced by my husband, who first introduced me to the subject of ecology when I was a student making a survey of our local salt marshes. His great knowledge of plants – especially of their natural habitats and associations – has been a fund on which I have drawn constantly throughout my life as a gardener and my career as a nurserywoman. That experience of looking closely at the plants of the salt marshes was an important step for me. But the most dramatic encounter with natural groupings of plants early in my adult life was when, a few years after we had married, we visited Switzerland. We were in the Valais in June and it was just like a garden, God's garden. I was bowled over. The plants looked so right in their places but even in a morning's scramblings we found quite different groupings, the plants of hot rocks and exposed positions such as *Dianthus* and *Helianthemum* being quite different in character to the campanulas, veratrums and yellow foxgloves of the cool north-facing slopes. The memory of those plant associations has coloured and influenced my gardening ever since.

Artistry in Planting

The artist Sir Cedric Morris, who died in 1982 at the age of 92, was another major influence on me. His stimulating company quickened my interest in many subjects and the breadth of his taste brought me into contact with many other fascinating people. To enter his garden was like going through a magic gate. I had never before seen such a range of plants as I discovered there. He was the leading private gardener in this part of East Anglia and at its peak his garden must have contained one of the largest collections of non-woody hardy plants in Britain. And they were planted by an artist. By that I do not mean that they were conventionally grouped in neat borders around contrived architectural features. There was an old walled garden but the planting extended beyond that with the design and reason of an artist's imagination.

Through Sir Cedric I was introduced to a wealth of plants of which I had previously been ignorant and, because he was so generous in giving me seeds and cuttings, many of these plants that were new discoveries for me found a place in my garden. I would never have become a nurserywoman had I not enjoyed a passion for propagating plants. When Sir Cedric gave me cuttings I practically took them to bed with me so anxious was I to get them to root; I didn't want to fail and have to ask for a replacement cutting.

My delight in propagating plants makes it difficult for me to embrace unreservedly the successes of micro-propagation. There is in me a tiny bit of resentment at the thought that micro-propagation could at a stroke supplant the techniques that it has taken forty years' experience – not to mention the accumulated knowledge passed on by others – to use effectively. To judge from the experience of the nursery, there is, however, still a great demand for the traditional skills of the propagator – and long may that continue.

Transforming a Wilderness

It was a luxury to be able to choose the site of our house and garden but most people seeing it before we started would not have thought it a luxury at all. There were none of the architectural features – walls, paving, steps and the like attractively softened by moss, lichens and ferns – that are sometimes thought of as prerequisites of the mature English garden. It was, quite simply, a wilderness – wasteland between

At White Barn Farm there is much to give encouragement to the gardener starting out with a difficult site. This garden has been created out of an overgrown wasteland between two farms, much of it consisting of dry gravel beds. The mature garden shows little evidence of this for it is now a beautifully assembled collection that pleases the most demanding plantsman or plantswoman. The associations which seem so natural are the result of skilful matching of plants to the conditions available.

37

two farms – with a soggy, spring-fed hollow running between gravel fields on either side. The boggy ground was overgrown with alders, willows and marsh thistles while the upper slopes were so dry that it was out of the question to try and farm them.

Most people looking at it would have considered that this land would never respond to cultivation. I knew though that, deserts and frozen wastes apart, there was no such thing as land where it was impossible to grow plants, and that, improbable though this piece of land was, there were plants suitable for the various conditions to be found in it. It was really a question of matching plants to conditions.

I could imagine sun-loving Mediterranean plants thriving on the hot gravel slopes and large-leaved plants like the giant gunneras combining with primulas and graceful grasses to make a lush water garden on the moist, heavy soil of the hollow. I could see, too, the makings of a woodland garden, with ferns, hostas, tiarellas and trilliums, if we could select a few trees that were worth saving and add to them with some imaginative planting.

When we started to make the garden we didn't work to a blueprint. There were many other demands on our time – we were still farming and bringing up a family – so we had to seize opportunities when they came. There was no help except on rare occasions when a man could be spared for a job.

Coping with the Climate

The major climatic factor, the low rainfall, was something we could do very little about. East Anglia is a very dry region and we live in a very dry part of it. The average annual rainfall is 50.8cm (20in) but on two occasions since we have been at White Barn Farm it has been as low as 40.6cm (16in). A couple of rainless months in a hot summer (cool summers suit us well) can spell disaster. We could, however, create a framework of trees and shrubs to give protection from the winds that blow from all quarters – in the winter and spring out of the Urals from the north-east and most of the summer across a 20ha (50 acre) field from the west. Creating a sheltered micro-climate is essential if your garden is situated as mine is in the middle of hundreds of acres of flat farmland and, in common with the rest of East Anglia, exposed to winds off the sea.

The Dry Garden

We started to develop the dry garden first because it was gardening in dry conditions that we knew most about. We had never had a bog garden or water garden and so had no experience of growing moisture-loving plants. From our previous garden we had brought a large number of drought-resistant plants – artemisias, asphodels, ballotas and verbascums, for example – which were held in nursery beds until they could be planted out.

Soil Improvement

The light gravelly soil was a pleasure to work after the heavy boulder clay I had been used to. It was the kind of soil I could get on at any time

The dry gravel slopes were the first part of the garden to be developed at White Barn Farm. The texture of the soil has been improved by the regular addition of copious quantities of organic material but another key to success has been the selection of drought-resistant plants, with the result that the slopes have a distinctly Mediterranean look.

of the year without fear of it becoming compacted. But it did need the addition of all the organic material such as leaf mould, farmyard manure and mushroom compost that I could get my hands on. Working it taught me an enormous amount about soil and how it can be improved with a little thought.

Perhaps my chief concern is for its texture, which is improved by adding well-rotted organic material. It is the micro-organisms working away in the soil, keeping it open and healthy, that you have to feed. I very rarely use concentrated fertilizers such as bonemeal, fish meal and their like. Adding fertilizers to the soil is like giving your plants little pills; it is much better to give them a really good meal. Where I tend to use fertilizers is in my tubs and pot gardens, of which I have a number arranged on paved areas. Plants growing in restricted conditions do get these little shots in the arm but I can't think of plants in the open garden that I feel ought to be given fertilizers in order to produce better flowers or foliage. In the dry garden especially, habit and foliage can develop quite uncharacteristically if plants get an unexpectedly rich diet of concentrated fertilizers.

Weeds and Mulches

When I first started, the weeding was phenomenal. Although the garden was a fraction of the size it is now, it was more than one could cope with. However, it wasn't really until the nursery was operating and I was employing a few local women to help with the weeding that I realized that this was not the best way for us to spend our time. I looked into the question of mulches and decided it was wiser to spend money on wages for propagating and expanding the nursery rather than on weeding; if mulches worked they wouldn't be just an expensive luxury, but really pay for themselves.

I started buying in peat but then discovered I could get crushed bark from a relatively nearby source. Bark was then still very little used as a mulch but it is not surprising that it has become popular. Its warm rough texture is very pleasing to look at, much more attractive to me than raked bare earth. It does gradually become incorporated in the soil and slowly rots away, but by the time it is beginning to get thin your plants are covering the ground. There will always be some hand weeding to do, but a mulch dramatically reduces the amount of weed that gets away and makes pleasurable whatever weeding is necessary. Weeds pull out of bark so easily and you don't take off all your topsoil in the process. If I didn't use mulches I would have to resort to chemical controls to keep the garden and nursery clear of weeds. I do use weedkillers but very selectively, mainly on paths and bare areas, rather than a planted one.

Another important benefit of mulching is that, provided the material is laid on soil that is not dry, it will help retain moisture and prevent run-off. Conserving moisture on my dry gravel slopes is very important. I make a good job of watering in when I am planting but once plants are established they are very rarely watered. Obviously if I have something choice I don't stand aside and let it die for lack of water but spot caring for individual plants is very different from standard irrigation. Obviously, the latter is a costly process and, I feel, unnecessary.

The reason I don't have irrigation in the garden (of course, the potted plants in the nursery have to be irrigated) is because I want to teach people how they can grow plants in the soil and conditions that they have. Most people can comfortably say that if Mrs Chatto can grow a plant they can as well – not find that they have bought a plant which they find impossible to grow on their home ground. Sometimes my Mediterranean plants are struggling but I don't lose anything. I would much rather see my grey plants bleached to whiteness by the drought, still alive although they may have retracted, than to change the character of the plants and the garden by irrigation.

Bark is not the only mulch I use but it is the one I prefer where the mulch is going to show, on the front edges and among the lower herbaceous plants. In the middle of really big borders I use straw. When it is first forked out the garden looks a bit like a farmyard but after it has had the weather on it, it becomes less conspicuous. I have been using straw on parts of the dry garden for twenty years and now have a really much improved soil. It is good on heavy clay, too. You don't damage the soil, leave unsightly footmarks or, for that matter, get the clay all over your boots. Other materials can also be used as mulches; with appropriate plants you can use rocks and pebbles. I have some raised beds in which I grow alpines and in these I use grit as a mulch.

What to Grow

The dry garden is far more rewarding than lots of people imagine and it is relevant in many situations, particularly the hot open gardens of new homes where there is no existing tree planting to cast shade. There are lots of plants you can't grow. It is no place for primulas or rhododendrons, or even more exotic plants such as the blue poppies (*Meconopsis*). But there are wonderful foliage plants that you can choose, plants with leaves that are adapted in a variety of ways to drought conditions.

For instance, they may be woolly, felted, wax-coated or leathery. Some, like *Crambe maritima* and *Verbascum olympicum*, have vast leaves and a few of these plants will keep the garden from looking fussy. A big leaf

A number of plants that do well in hot dry parts of the garden have silvery or grey-green leaves. However, artemisias, ballotas and santolinas, among others, need to be used with discretion. A garden that features grey foliage alone can seem formless and dull.

acts as a fullstop, a point where the eye rests, and that is as important as a lively mixture of contrasting detail.

Tonal Values

The greys and silvery tones are often very beautiful, especially when you see them shining out in the half light of a summer evening. Many of the grey-leaved plants –including ballotas, helichrysums, lavenders and santolinas –make attractive mounds, cushions or buns, the shape of one plant merging with that of another. A meagre diet and some judicious pruning when older plants get leggy will help to keep the growth tight. However, if you have only plants with grey foliage, the garden can look like an ash heap. You need to introduce different colour tones, for example with some of the rock roses. *Cistus ladanifer* has narrow, dark green leaves and a large shrub of it makes a good contrast to silvers and greys. Its crumpled white flowers are handsomely marked at the base with purple-black blotches. The jagged leaves of yuccas provide another contrast that is interesting at any time of the year and when these plants produce their spires of waxy flowers they are truly magnificent.

Although foliage is the most important element in the dry garden, furnishing it almost as densely in winter as in summer, many of the shrubby plants do have interesting, if not conspicuous, flowers. But flower colour comes not just from shrubby plants; a succession of bulbs and herbaceous plants such as pinks make their seasonal contributions to overall effect.

It is sometimes said of my planting that the colour schemes are soft but that is simply in the nature of the plants I grow. Few species plants have large flamboyant flowers; if I introduce cultivars, I avoid those with bright brassy colours. Other than that I don't aim for colour effects. I don't specifically try to make a white garden or a red garden. The colour schemes come and go with the seasons.

Grouping Plants

I often refer to the nucleus of my dry garden as my 'Mediterranean Garden', because so many of the plants that are grouped there are Mediterranean in origin. Many belong to the *maquis* or *garigue*, the more or less stable plant communities that have survived following the destruction of the evergreen forests that once clothed the stony hillsides of southern Europe. I have grouped such plants as the magnificent *Euphorbia wulfenii*, which gives the garden an unmistakably southern character, around a core of trees that include *Cupressus sempervirens*, *Juniperus communis* and *Taxus baccata* 'Fastigiata'. Aromatic plants such as lavenders, rock roses, rosemary and rue emphasize the Mediterranean theme. But with the Mediterranean natives I grow plants from dry areas in other parts of the world – the western United States, for instance – as well. *Artemisia purshiana* and *Zauschneria californica* are from the Californian chaparral; *Crambe cordifolia* from the Caucasus; hebes and *Senecio* 'Sunshine' from New Zealand; and galtonias and nerines from Southern Africa. The result is a coherent grouping of plants, all requiring similar conditions.

Drought Resistant Plants

In another dry area I am growing drought-resistant plants on a much bigger scale. I have a large border by the drive entrance where, for example, I am growing drifts of *Phlomis russeliana*, rock roses and large patches of oriental poppies. Among these and other flowering plants I am growing large numbers of grasses, some tall growing such as *Stipa gigantea*, but also smaller kinds such as *Festuca glauca* and *Helichtotrichon sempervirens*, both with blue foliage. One of the loveliest grasses we now have is *Deschampsia caespitosa* 'Goldschleier' (golden veil), which has airy plumes that turn from silvery green to bright straw yellow. Grasses are not yet given their full credit but eventually they will be recognized as some of the most beautiful and useful plants to set among drought-

Despite the dry climate of East Anglia, many woodland plants that enjoy dappled shade grow well at White Barn Farm. There are even fern species that thrive, provided that they are planted in pockets of moisture-retentive soil and sheltered from drying winds.

resistant plants, making an ideal contrast to those with felted or leathery leaves and compact habit.

Although an important reason for choosing the site at White Barn Farm was the possibility of making a water garden in the permanently damp hollow, I have never failed to get pleasure from gardening on our really dry gravelly soils. One of the best pieces of publicity the nursery has ever had came from an article written by Graham Rose after he had visited the garden during a period when we were experiencing a protracted drought. He was impressed not so much by the lush growth in the wet hollow but by the plants holding out against the drought on our hot dry slopes. He recognized that there was a lesson here from which many gardeners could profit.

The Woodland Garden

We began the woodland garden almost at the same time as we started gardening on the dry gravel slopes. We had had a bulldozer in to clear away a lot of the rubbish but saved one or two mature trees. Nonetheless the clearing left us with a very bare site and more trees had to be planted. As with most people planting a garden, our enthusiasm ran away with us and we put in far more trees than there was room for. We soon realized that in an area of low rainfall such as ours, too many trees meant a canopy of foliage keeping water from reaching the ground and stiff competition from tree roots for woodland shrubs and perennials.

What this meant, we came to realize, was that we had to change and adapt our original ideas. We had to strike a balance between clothing the landscape with a few trees of good height but not so many that would make it difficult to grow plants on the ground. Quite a few trees from our initial planting had to come out.

Back to Soil Improvement

In the early stages we didn't realize what a problem we had with the soil under the trees but our failures indicated that something was amiss. The trouble, we found, was that in this part of our land there was no structure to the soil. It was extraordinarily silty, not quite as dense and solid as clay but with such fine particles that the air couldn't get into it. It had not been disturbed for generations and you could even smell that it was stale. When it dried out it became as fine as face powder and then when it rained the water would just run off; it couldn't penetrate the soil under the trees at all.

I found that the way to give this curiously lifeless soil structure – and therefore channels through which air and water could pass freely – was to add not only bulky organic matter but also grit. Pea-sized grit was the most suitable material, but we also used gravel that we had excavated in other parts of the garden.

A Different Climate
Even on a very small scale it is possible to create a woodland garden. Once we had got the soil right, we found that there were wonderful

things we could grow, despite the dry climate of East Anglia. It is almost as though, when we stand on cool moisture-retentive soil beneath the trees, we experience a different climate to that which is found in the 'Mediterranean Garden'.

Ferns

In the moist western counties of Britain there would be far more scope for growing ferns, the most characteristic foliage plants of woodland. Here we need to give them shelter from desiccating winds and to grow them in pockets well filled with compost or leaf mould to retain moisture. One very easy species, the male fern (*Dryopteris filix-mas*), will grow in hedge bottoms in the most mean places. In more favourable conditions it can almost become a weed but here we are glad to have its divided deep green leaves. The common polypody (*Polypodium vulgare*), which in wetter counties is a common roadside plant, is not often seen growing wild in East Anglia. We have the finely cut variety 'Cornubiense'. One of our loveliest successes is an elegant form of the soft shield fern, *Polystichum setiferum* 'Acutilobum', a luxuriant grower in cool semi-shade.

The delicate pattern of ferns is wonderfully contrasted against bold shapes such as the broad leaves of hostas. I have seen hostas planted with blue rue but that is something I would never do. I see the hosta as a plant for the shady ferny side of the garden whereas rue belongs with the grey-leaved plants of the dry garden. If you want large leaves in the dry garden you can use *Crambe maritima* or bergenias, which have leathery leaves that are much better equipped to withstand drought than the leaves of hostas.

Ground Cover

Excellent ground-covering plants to combine with ferns and hostas include ajugas, epimediums, Solomon's seal (*Polygonatum*), tiarellas and *Tellima*. The North American *T. grandiflora* 'Purpurea' has round scalloped leaves that are with you all year round, turning rich purple and bronze in winter. Not all the epimediums are evergreen but some, such as *E. × rubrum*, hold on to their heart-shaped leaves in the winter creating pinky-bronze patches in the garden. Most epimediums are best cut down in early March to reveal the delicate sprays of small flowers.

A more typically European woodland plant is the foxglove. Although I love the common form of *Digitalis purpurea* in the wild, I weed it out in the garden because I don't want it to cross with white, cream and primrose forms. In the summer when leaves are showing but no flowers you can tell those that will flower purple from the purple staining of the leaf base. 'Sutton's Yellow', a primrose yellow, is a particularly desirable form that I like to see seeding itself naturally, coming up between shrubs and other things. There are perennial foxgloves that I grow, too: *D. grandiflora* and *D. lutea* with yellow flowers and *D. × mertonensis* with strawberry-pink spikes.

Bulbs

It is often forgotten that there are excellent bulbs for woodland conditions. *Cyclamen hederifolium*, for example, tolerates shade and even quite dry conditions and yet produces a good crop of elegant flowers. The silvered and mottled foliage is especially welcome in winter and spring. When I began, I made the mistake of planting them with vincas; these ran all over the cyclamen, so I have now learned to keep them planted apart.

These cyclamen are autumn flowering but it is the early spring bulbs that give the garden a lift when the year is starting dark and cold. You can never tire of snowdrops and wood anemones (I grow selected forms of *Anemone nemorosa* such as the coal blue 'Allenii' and the large blue 'Robinsoniana'). Some of the species narcissi are suitable for woodland conditions and all the American eythroniums are worth growing. I wouldn't want to be without the European dog's-tooth violet (*Erythronium dens-canis*), with its blotched leaves and lily-like flowers. Lilies are the main summer bulbs of woodland, most enjoying deep moist soil and dappled light. But the North American camassias are another group worth planting if you have sunny gaps.

Rhododendrons, the classic woodland plants of the Himalayas, are not prominently represented at White Barn Farm – they do much better on acid soils in moister parts of the country. But many geographical

Even in late winter and early spring there are interesting plants to see in the woodland garden. Snowdrops are always welcome and here they grow among *Helleborus corsicus* and *Arum italicum* 'Pictum'.

45

areas of the temperate world are represented in our woodland areas. Plants from the Americas, China, Europe and Japan grow together without jarring because they are all species and forms that require very similar conditions. Our plant associations may be man-created but they are convincing because they take into account the natural habitats of the constituents.

The Water Garden

The water garden was not an afterthought, but it required time and money to develop and so was not part of the first phase of our garden making here. We started with the great advantage of having running water, a spring-fed ditch running through the centre of the hollow. Even in very bad droughts, when there has been no rain for three or four months, this ditch has never dried out. Another, although mixed, blessing was that beneath the meadow silt was clay. To make ponds, we only needed to excavate holes to a sufficient depth and to build up dams with appropriate outflows. There was no need to line the ponds, or carry out other expensive work – or so we thought.

A False Start

In the event, making the ponds was not as simple as we expected. The first two ponds were excavated by a contractor using a dragline. We didn't have them made very deep because we were put off by the problem of disposing of piles of clay; most of what was taken out was used to create the dams.

Our main mistake, however, was to start planting almost as soon as the soil had begun to settle. The native moisture-loving plants, such as sedges and rushes, were all there and they came up promptly and finished, but the plants I wanted to grow hated being in brick-making clay and so stubbornly refused to thrive.

Preparing the Soil

After a few years of hard work but unsatisfactory results I decided that, with more help and a little more money, it would be worth starting the water garden again. This time I took a lot longer over preparing the soil, taking away some of the clay and bringing in lighter soil, including nursery waste, compost and leafmould. You can't always take clay away because of the problem of disposal but you can bring in lighter soil and put it on top of the clay.

If you can build up a foot, preferably more, of good soil on top, moisture from the clay will come up through it. Plants will get their nourishment from the humus-rich top layer and, once they are established in the soil, they will get their roots down into the clay.

Removing the Ponds

Most of the giant lush herbaceous plants in the water garden die away completely in the winter months but the short period of decline has its own rich beauty.

Over twenty-seven years, the ponds gradually began to silt up, so I decided they must be dredged with a dragline to remove accumulated leaves and waste material. I expected chaos but by the spring you would hardly know that anything had happened. The scraping out was done with the ponds undrained. As soon as the work began, the water

became muddied and the contractor was, in a sense, working blind. It sounds very inefficient but the man knew what he was doing. The ponds are now much deeper in the centre but there is still a shallow rim around the edge for my plants.

What to Grow

The one part of the garden that is tropically lush all summer dies away almost completely in winter. *Phormium tenax* (unless the weather is very severe) and some of the carex species remain standing but almost all the herbaceous plants, including giants such as the gunneras, vanish. Sometimes in the off-season visitors ask me why I have taken everything out.

Perhaps it is because I am an East Anglian who has struggled for so many years to grow lush-looking plants that the sheer healthy bulk of foliage is what gives me most pleasure in the water garden. I love the massive leaves of gunneras, large enough to shelter under, the spinach-like leaves of *Lysichitum americanum*, some as tall as I am, and the great swords of *Phormium tenax*, often six feet high. Large spaces need large plants; without some strong statements the garden can look bitty. However, don't force these large plants into inappropriately small gardens. The lysichitums, for example, are not suitable for growing in artifical ponds. They must be able to get their roots down – and they will go down several feet.

The flower spathes of the lysichitons appear before the leaves and are among the first things to show in the bare mud early in spring. *L. americanum* is bright yellow but *L. camtschatcense* is pure white. They are followed by the marsh marigolds (*Caltha palustris*) and primulas, beginning with the magenta-red *P.japonica*. As the growing season picks up, a wealth of plants comes into flower: globe flowers (*Trollius*), *Lysimachia*, *Lythrum*, astilbes and rudbeckias, which carry on into the autumn. But I don't like too much colour in the water garden; I like to see a lot of foliage separating the colour, so I really welcome the great surge of leafy growth after the first flowers of spring. I have already mentioned plants with large leaves; a lovely contrast to them is the arching foliage of grasses such as *Miscanthus sinensis* in its various forms. As elsewhere in the garden, I don't set out to create specific colour schemes or to have colour everywhere all the time. I am much happier planting a group of one colour or of harmonizing colours and to set that against quiet areas where nothing is flowering at all.

Reservoir Planting

Around the home ponds, I have taken a great deal of trouble to improve the soil so that I can grow fine herbaceous plants. From my early mistake I learned that unless I did that I couldn't expect good results. Around the reservoir that sits at the edge of the property I adopted a different approach. This was like many sheets of water so often neglected by landowners but easily improved by planting. I decided that the plants here would have to look after themselves so I have put in tough and hardy shrubs and trees. Metasequoias and taxodiums, silver birches and willows have all flourished.

One herbaceous plant that has no trouble growing in the solid plasticine clay of the reservoir's surrounds is *Petasites japonicus* 'Giganteus'. It is an aggressive plant that is almost frightening in its vigour. I would not want it anywhere else in the garden but I am glad to have it here. In no part of the garden is the planting static and this is as true of the reservoir area as anywhere else. I don't want it to require time-consuming hand maintenance but I have added to my original planting of trees and shrubs a number of the coarser herbaceous plants, including bergenias.

Past and Present

Perhaps it is just as well that in the early 1960s we did not know what would be involved in transforming our unpromising site into the gardens as they now are. Then I was simply fired with an enthusiasm to grow a wide range of interesting and unusual plants, and I was delighted to have in my garden contrasting conditions that allowed me to accommodate associations of very different character and requirements. I may have become obsessed with the improvement of the different kinds of soil contained in this relatively small piece of land but I have never wanted to grow plants in wholly artifical situations and so I have never set out to change fundamentally the character of any part of the garden. What I *have* tried to do – I hope successfully and by learning from all my experiences – is to observe and work from an understanding of the soil as it is but, improving it to provide the best conditions that I can to ensure the vigorous healthy growth of plants suited to it. As there must be in any garden, there have been failures. But, in the main, plant groupings have been successful beyond our early expectations, giving enormous pleasure and serving, I hope, as a source of ideas and inspiration for other gardeners.

The water garden was the last area to be developed at White Barn Farm and proved the most troublesome. The ponds were excavated in a spring-fed hollow; after passing through the garden this natural water supply finds its way to a small reservoir on the edge of the property.

Planting for Colour

CHRISTOPHER LLOYD

The garden at Great Dixter, Christopher Lloyd's family home in East Sussex, is famous for its rare and beautiful plants, which have been brought together with an artistry that does not shy away from exuberant effects. From spring to autumn, it is a garden of rich and exciting colours, but with many subtleties, too, that might escape the casual visitor.

In February, when I interviewed Mr Lloyd, the garden showed a facet of its character that might come as a surprise to anyone who has revelled in its bold juxtapositions of summer colour. On a bitter overcast day, when almost all colour had been reduced to monochromatic tones – even the first crocuses, winter aconites and snowdrops hardly showed – the massive yew hedges gave the garden a splendid solemn beauty. The effect is not over-solemn, however, for the yew topiary has a homeliness about it that seems at one in character with the house itself.

Those who only know this exciting garden in full summer can now get some idea of its full seasonal range for Christopher Lloyd, one of the most stimulating modern writers on gardening, has recently published a new book, *The Year at Great Dixter*. Whatever he has to say about his own or any other garden is worth noting.

In the Long Border at Great Dixter – a mixed border in which shrubs, roses, perennials, bulbs and even annuals rub shoulders – Christopher Lloyd allows all the colours, but not all of them together. Foliage plants are particularly important in separating difficult colours.

MOST PEOPLE living in northern Europe feel that as so much of the year is dark, and the sky is so often a great canopy of cloud, that we do need some bright colour around to cheer us up. Some may consider the colourfulness of bedding-out schemes in parks and the planting of front gardens a bit vulgar. Many more welcome the relief from the drabness not only of the skies but also very often of their lives.

As people become more sophisticated they tend to shy away from what they consider to be rather obvious, perhaps influenced by friends or visitors who convey in their critical remarks the judgement of

prevailing fashion. Or perhaps a visit to a famous garden like the celebrated garden Vita Sackville-West and her husnabd, Sir Harold Nicolson, created at Sissinghurst, in Kent, makes such an impression on visitors that it has a lasting influence on them – the white garden, for example, is taken as a model for the garden at home.

Little Sissinghurst, can be seen all over the place; I saw one recently as far away as North Carolina in the American South. But a word of caution. Gardening in the Sissinghurst style is perfectly valid, but it should never be followed slavishly.

Fashion really is a dirty word for me because people think that only what is fashionable is right. We can't help being swayed by fashion but it should never be the tail that wags the dog. The great thing is to have a wide range of tastes, to enjoy every colour and to realize that there is no such thing as a bad colour. It is just a question of how and where you use them. Use every sort of colour and enjoy it, not minding too much what other people say.

Dark and Pale Colours

There are various ways in which you can help yourself to use colour most effectively. One way is to remember that the dark rich colours, the purples and reds, the deep reds especially, are best viewed from close range, with the light behind you. Then they are exciting. Do not construct the whole of your garden to be seen from a distance, from your sitting-room windows, for instance. Although that view is very important because you probably spend a lot more time indoors looking out at your garden than you do actually in the garden itself, for highest enjoyment of these richer colours you need to be close to them.

Pale and Interesting

The pale colours are the ones that look best from a distance. I deal a lot in clematis and I am always being asked to recommend these climbers for different situations, so I always think of this point in relation to them. A light blue clematis like 'Perle d'Azur' is going to be most effective in the garden scene. This is borne out at Sissinghurst Castle, where they grow clematis so well. They have a wonderful display on a curved wall: stand back from that and you can see a great curtain of 'Perle d'Azur'. It is effective enough close up but it shows up particularly well at a distance. If in the same position they had used, say, 'Royal Velours' – a sumptuous deep velvety red clematis – you would need to be close to it and with the sun shining quite brightly to get the same excitement.

Light and Shade

Whether you see plants with the light behind you or with the light behind them makes a great difference. The translucent foliage of purple-leaved forms of the smoke bush (*Cotinus coggygria*) shines like rubies when the light is behind it at the beginning or end of the day. It is worth taking trouble over the placing of plants such as the smoke bush or some of the yellow-leaved shrubs. *Philadelphus coronarius* 'Aureus', for example, has young foliage of a very tender glowing yellow. If grown against a dark, north-facing wall, the high sunlight coming over onto the young foliage in May will show it up well against the dark backcloth of the wall.

Some colours show up especially well at certain times of the day. At Glyndebourne, which is visited mostly in the evening by opera-goers, and seen then and at night, it is clear that pale colours are going to suit. So they have borders of white flowers combined with pale grey foliage. Towards sunset reds take on an added lustre, almost as though they have their own source of light. The volcanic glow of reds and oranges is very exciting but these colours go quite black when night descends.

Green is the most dominant colour in the garden. Foliage is much longer lasting than flowers and in Britain, because grass grows particularly well in our climate, the lawn is a favourite adjunct to borders, beds and flowers. Green is quite a strong colour, or tends to be strong, and this should be taken into account when planting beds and borders near by. Sometimes, the bright green of a lawn detracts from the effect of flowers in a way that neutral, sand-coloured paving would not. This is particularly so with pale, soft colours like pinks, greys and whites. Green can help, though, when you are using bright colours. It throws up strong orange and red.

Many shades of White

White borders and white gardens seem to be particularly popular at the moment. If you make a white bed or a white garden, don't be too rigid. Grey should also count as white, and pale green flowers will mix in very well. At Sissinghurst, the white garden includes pale green flowers and glaucous foliage. The most exciting foliage plant is *Melianthus major*, a South African species that has big pinnate leaves, jagged at the edge, and with a marvellous bluish bloom.

Another Sissinghurst departure from pure white is *Rosa serafinii*, a species with aromatic foliage that perfumes the air rather like our own sweet briar. It has white flowers, followed late in the season by little scarlet hips. The purist might cut off the hips to prevent them spoiling the whiteness of the garden but I think it is absolutely right to leave them, as they are left at Sissinghurst, giving a little relief.

Do not grow many of the very dead white flowers, such as certain of

A white border, dominated by delphiniums, includes the grey-green foliage of an artemisia, which helps to soften the overall impression. The popularity of white borders probably owes something to well-known examples such as the 'white garden' at Sissinghurst Castle. There the white is relieved by pale green flowers and plenty of foliage, glaucous as well as green.

the white phloxes and the white shasta daisy (*Leucanthemum maximum*). The funereal white of the flowers is not helped by the heavy green of the leaves. The single shastas with a yellow centre are much easier to deal with than the doubles, which are white all through. Choose flowers in which the whiteness is modulated, as it is in the snowdrop, which has touches of green in it, or as in other cases when the white is creamy.

Combining Colours

Personally, I do not think I would ever make a white garden. I would rather offset my white flowers with other colours. One of the best combinations is with yellow. This occurs in many flowers already, as in members of the daisy family. Yellow and white combinations can include yellow foliage plants as well as yellow-flowered ones. The cut-leaved yellow elder (*Sambucus racemosa* 'Plumosa Aurea'), a plant which I wouldn't be without, is particularly useful because it tolerates quite a lot of shade. A snag with yellow-foliaged plants is that a lot of them scorch in hot sunlight but this can be avoided if you give them plenty of water or a little shade. After all, we want good plants for shady situations because every garden needs shade as well as sun.

Exciting Contrasts

Yellow with orange or red gives a very much hotter effect that has its place too and is one that, with a lawn surround, works terribly well. I

At Barnsley House in Gloucestershire, a garden full of stimulating ideas, a border of predominantly warm colours is gently cooled by the inclusion of touches of white and the glossy green foliage of bergenias.

remember seeing an example of this in John Treasure's garden at Tenbury Wells. He had brilliant orange crocosmias and yellow yarrows. (*Achillea filipendulina* 'Coronation Gold') and also, I think, red hot pokers (*Kniphofia*). These were toned down by the white bells of the Cape hyacinth (*Galtonia candicans*) and set off by the surrounding greens.

I thought it was very successful, particularly where the crocosmias were hanging over the green lawn, but the owner had tired of it and wanted a change. These hot colours are rather tiring, particularly if you are living with them all the time. They are very exciting but then, too much excitement wears a bit thin.

There is no doubt that the hot colours, bright oranges and reds, are the ones that people are most frightened of handling. I think that they are missing out on something, for it is all a matter of how they are used. For instance, in a recent television programme on Glyndebourne it was pointed out that an orange daisy, *Anthemis sancti-johannis*, introduced by me to the garden, was not entirely successful. I admit that one patch that did not relate to anything in particular was rather startling. But in another part the gardener had used it most effectively in double mixed borders interplanted with the yellow shrub rose 'Chinatown'. The spotty impression that the rose might have created was avoided by linking the planting with a raised carpet of anthemis.

A supreme example of the inspirational use of hot colours is at Hidcote, in Gloucestershire. In the double red borders they use red foliage and the purple-leaved forms of *Cotinus coggygria* and *Berberis thunbergii*,as well as red flowers, together with glaucous foliage like *Melianthus major*, which tones down the reds but also serves to subtly accentuate them.

What interests me about red borders is that they must be mixed borders. You can't just rely on herbaceous plants because there are not a great many herbaceous plants with red flowers and they do not flower for very long. For example, the Maltese cross (*Lychnis chalcedonica*), has domes of startling vermilion scarlet flowers . It is a very good shape and you can make contrasts and harmonies with it, but after two weeks in July it is done for. You can perhaps afford to carry a few passengers if you have very big borders but not in a small garden. In the hot range I have a very good form of *Crocosmia masonorum* — 'Dixter Flame' — that is useful for it flowers for quite three weeks, with the individual flowers presented elegantly on the top of the curved panicle. However, its flowering season is unusually long for a flower of this colour.

Roses in Mixed Borders
Roses are a great help wherever you want to introduce red in a mixed border. One I use a lot in my long, mixed border is 'Florence May Morse'. It is not a subtle rose, it hasn't a particularly well-shaped flower, but it is a double and it does not show the centre at all. It flowers twice and is a very pure, clean, straightforward red without any blue in it and it is a good colour for a mixed or red border.

I like to integrate roses in mixed borders as an important but not overriding element, with other shrubs, herbaceous perennials, bulbs, annuals, bedding plants and tender perennials.

Although I have a rose garden of my own I would never make one if I was starting from scratch. Roses are frequently used as a substitute for bedding out for the simple reason that bedding out has to be done twice a year whereas roses can be left for a number of years. But they do not do the same job by any manner of means. In fact, it seems to me that they do the job extremely unsatisfactorily. Because of the spottiness of their flowers they never make the sort of impact that you need from bedding. They underdo the impact whereas something like *Salvia splendens*, with its congested colour, overdoes it. The trouble with the hybrid teas and the floribunda, is that the structure of the shrub is makeshift, just a number of sticks. Unless it is very closely covered with flowers you are aware of the bad shape of the plant itself.

Purples and Blues

If planting purple and mauve borders, remember that these look glum under a grey sky so you will not want to look at them much except when the sun is shining. I feel this about the purple and mauve plantings at Sissinghurst, just inside the gateway. Some large bushes of *Rosa moyesii* that were there, I think I am right in saying, before the borders were planned to be all purple and mauve, have scarlet hips in August. It helps a lot to have a little bit of a break.

Blue is probably the most popular colour of all, yet, when you come to think of it, there are not many pure blue flowers. We often flatter with the name of blue a flower which has quite a bit of mauve in it, as we are forced to do with clematis like 'Lasurstern' or 'Perle d'Azur', simply because there are so many other clematis that are obviously mauve or purple.

Pure blue, is particularly valued. We find it in cynoglossums (*Cynoglossum amabile* 'Bluebird' is a true blue), delphiniums, forget-me-nots (although they often have a touch of pink) and blue salvias like *Salvia patens*. These are intensely exciting colours. I think we love them because they remind us of blue skies, which we need so much in our climate. However, it is a mistake, in my view, to make a border of nothing but blue flowers. Blue needs lifting by other colours; used alone it becomes extraordinarily dull. It really is a waste of a most valuable colour. Plant deep blue delphiniums, for instance, with pink peonies, — great double fat pink ones. Not only do they look marvellous together in the garden if you have room for a border that is distinctly seasonal and will not do much for you later on, but they also look good in flower arrangements.

Blues with yellows look lovely, especially if they are soft blues and soft yellows. They go well, too, with whites. But blues with mauves are not so good. Gertrude Jekyll realized that this was so in her famous mixed border – she called it a mixed border but in retrospect everyone calls it a herbaceous border — she started off with blues at one end and finished with mauves at the other. But she did not put these colours together; though they were playing the same role, they were playing it at different extremities of the border.

Bedding Schemes

A great advantage of bedding over the semi-permanent planting of mixed or herbaceous borders is that you can experiment freely with

Dahlias have been used here in a hot but simple colour scheme of red and orange in the National Trust garden at Anglesey Abbey, Cambridgeshire. Many bedding plants, including dahlias, are often grown in mixtures but the jumbling of bright colours can be very agitating to the eye.

colour combinations. You never have to do the same thing twice or worry about making mistakes because these can be rectified the following year. You can even make a change two or three times in a year. It is great fun experimenting with colours, textures, heights and flowering seasons. So be adventurous and avoid repeating combinations, even when you have done something well. There is very little more rewarding than continual experimentation.

Resist a Riot

One thing to guard against is the speckling colours, dotting them about. This is partly the plantsman in us that wants to grow as many different plants as possible in a small area. When people are very clever at growing plants from seed and from cuttings they tend to make an absolute riot of colour. Even gardens where enormous pains have been taken to get a wonderful display that will go on for many weeks are spoiled by this fidgetiness, the colours cancelling one another out. It is far more effective to arrange the colours in group plantings.

Dot plants used to tone down the colour of bedding schemes, are also best in groups. Despite its unremitting scarlet, people do use *Salvia splendens* to make great displays but they generally realize that it has got to be broken up in some way or another, so they put in dot plants, which are usually grey or purple foliage. These would look a lot better grouped so that instead of making dots they made, say, a background of quiet foliage. If the foliage of cannas, for example, has got to be among the flowers, make quite a broad expanse of it. Cannas have beautiful leaves, smooth-textured and broad like paddles and they can be green,

Mixtures need to be treated with some caution. In the case of bedding plants there are often too many colours, creating in the mass a very agitating impression. This is particularly so when individual flowers contain several colours. However, mixtures with a limited range of shades, as in the case of these helianthemums, can be very effective.

purple or green and purple. Even if cannas don't flower very well in the British climate they make good plants, especially when grown with scarlet dahlias. Both form good-sized patches.

A lot of annuals and other bedding plants have a mixture of colours in one flower and that again can be fidgety. When choosing sweet williams I don't go for the auricula-eyed variety. Although pretty at close range, at a distance they present a blurred effect. It is the same with pansies and violas. If planting a window box, a tub or a trough that you will see close to, the ones with faces are excellent, but if you are making a planting to be seen from a distance – as it were a carpet for tulips or a bedding scheme – then single-coloured pansies are much the best.

Sympathetic Mixtures
Some seed mixtures are good because they combine relatively few shades. For example, a mixture of penstemmons for a late summer display will all be in shades of red, pink, mauve and purple. All of these colours harmonize and the mixture will be effective. But if you go for a mixture of polyanthus, say, you may be in trouble because there are too many colours. There are bright pinks as well as bright reds, bright oranges and bright yellows and they do not all look well together. The yellow centre can be bred out of the polyanthus, but normally the flower has a large, central yellow flash and then a colour outside that. The combination looks particularly good if you have a white polyanthus, which is then a white and yellow flower, or a yellow polyanthus, which is a flower in two shades of yellow. An orange polyanthus, too, can be a happy combination of a hot colour with a quieter tone. Suttons used to do a very good mixture called 'Brilliancy', which are shades of orange and flame, all the flowers having yellow centres. There was also blue polyanthus with yellow centres, although blue is a dark, sulky shade. This colour must be seen from close to.

Too Many Colours
Antirrhinums and dahlias, as well as polyanthus, are difficult because commercial mixtures include an excessive number of colours. It is better to make your own mixtures, although separate colours are not always easy to get. This is the case with the antirrhinum, a flower I very much like to use for bedding schemes. One year I might make a mixture of flame, orange and white, and another year of pink, red, carmine, magenta and perhaps white again. Antirrhinums make beautiful regular spikes but the flowers themselves are irregular in shape.

The most popular mixtures of wallflowers also include too many colours. People think that a packet of mixed seed is the best value for money because they will have something of everthing. Resist this very human reaction and aim to have different colours in different years. Fortunately it is still relatively easy to get separate colours in wall-flowers. If planning to combine them with tulips, don't dot the tulips about among the wallflowers. Plant patches of wallflowers so that every plant touches its neighbour. The wallflower, after all, is not a pretty plant. But en masse they are very attractive. Plant a mass of wallflowers and then a mass of tulips in front or in the centre, or behind them. Probably it will most often be behind the wallflowers because, generally speaking, most tulips are taller than most wallflowers. Again, use single colours of tulips rather than mixtures.

Personal Choice

This coming summer I plan to plant a bedding phlox, a strain of *Phlox drummondii* called 'Beauty Mixed'. What I like about this strain is that there are no clashing colours. Although all the colours are rather intense, there is only one colour in each plant.

Many *Phlox drummondii* strains have a mixture of colour within each flower. But with 'Beauty Mixed' you get contrasts from plant to plant, not within the same plant, and each specimen is big enough to make quite an impression. I think it will look pretty good with a background of quiet Japanese anemones. These flower from the end of July until the middle of October, which is very useful in a herbaceous perennial. Each flower has a beautiful shape, with a green cone in the centre surrounded by yellow stamens and white petals. The combination of white, yellow and green makes a good background to any kind of bedding, even if it is another white flower. There is enough contrast in the anemones to provide the necessary variety.

Colour in Naturalized Planting

When naturalizing bulbs such as daffodils and narcissi there is always a temptation, which is encouraged by the commercial firms selling the bulbs, to plant what is called a 'mixture for naturalizing'. I always

In the daffodil orchard at Great Dixter most of the hybrids grown are kinds that were fashionable in the early part of this century. As a rule, these are more refined than the modern cultivars. Drifts are planted in single varieties; mixtures look confused.

suspect that this consists of any bulbs that are left over and need to be got rid of. These mixtures give you many different varieties, which you may think is an advantage, but they always look bitty when seen from a distance. What is more, different bulbs will flower at different times.

I don't think I could improve on what was done in my own garden before the First World War. The yellows and whites were kept separate, trumpet daffodils such as 'Emperor' grouped distinctly from yellow narcissi such as 'Barrii Conspicuus'. All the varieties are pre-First World War, but it doesn't matter that they are old or out of date. In fact, the old varieties are not as coarse and muscular as the modern ones; the fact that they haven't been 'improved' to the same extent as varieties popular now is really to their advantage.

It is not totally a matter of colour, although this comes into it. When naturalizing daffodils and narcissi, do not plant them too thickly. William Robinson, who in the nineteenth century vigorously encouraged gardeners to naturalize plants rather than to grow them formally, said that when planting daffodils one should study the formation of a cloud, how it is denser in the centre and more fragmented at the edge. Most important of all, leave plenty of grass between the groups. Think of daffodils in the same way you would waterlilies in a pond. You want to see the surface of the water; that is the whole point of a pond. The point of an orchard full of daffodils is the grass. It will be sufficient to devote a third or quarter of the area to waterlilies or to bulbs, leaving the grass or water in between for you to enjoy in its own right.

A Bold Approach to Colour

The combination of what are generally considered to be clashing colours – oranges, brilliant reds, pinks and magentas of a tub of geraniums – can go surprisingly well together.

The busy lizzies (*Impatiens*) provide another case where, as a gardener of ours used to say, the colours clash well. They present the most improbable juxtapositions of red, orange, pink, magenta and white. However, they all tend to be on the pink side of white, only the orange containing a hint of yellow.

Yellow and pink is generally thought to be a bad combination. I am quite sure that one could make a successful pink and yellow border if one set about it and I would really like to do this some time. You would have to avoid solid blocks of colour; a solid block of bright pink next to another of mustard yellow like *Achillea filipendulina* 'Coronation Gold' would obviously be a disaster. So would the rose 'Zéphirine Drouhin', which is a shocking pink, next to 'Coronation Gold'. But pale pinks with pale yellows, or even bright pinks with bright yellows but small flowers, could be most attractive separated by grey foliage or by flowering grasses so that the effect was fragmented.

In California recently I was particularly struck by this combination in wild flowers. There you have wild Californian poppies (*Eschscholzia*), which are either orange or yellow, mixed with wild clarkias, which are quite indisputably pink, sometimes with a touch of mauve, which makes the combination even more difficult. However, there is sand in between and there are grasses so that the effect never looks excessive. One needs to think of what will soften the colours.

61

Borders at Great Dixter

At Dixter, I have no colour schemes apart from my bedding out, which is changed every year and where I do think of my colour schemes individually. In the main borders, which are all mixed, I allow all the colours but not all of them together. When planting, I always try to think of what I am putting next to something. Sometimes I am deceived or forget. For instance, I have planted 'Tessa', a rather pucey pink early-flowering rhododendron, in a border where I knew it would do well, forgetting entirely the presence of a carpet of a brilliant orange-yellow crocus, *Crocus aureus*. The two did not go well together. Mind you, in the spring, in the early part of the season particularly, you can get away with what you would call a clash in summer, because there is so much bare ground and so little colour about at all. The clash is almost welcome because it is a gladdening sight in the garden after all the dreary winter months. Nevertheless, I had to admit that this was a mistake and I have moved the crocuses to another part of the garden.

Foliage Colours

In my mixed borders, foliage plays a very great part – acting as a solvent for bright colours. It is much more difficult to make mistakes if you have good foliage colours and shapes. I think of foliage colours as much as flower colours. For instance, I have Dickson's golden elm (*Ulmus carpinifolia sarniensis* 'Aurea') at the back of the border. It is about the tallest plant in the border, almost a tree, but every other year we clip it over to prevent it becoming uncontrollable. That is behind a pale silvery willow called *Salix alba* 'Argentea'. Between them these two give sustenance, so to speak, for a large part of the summer. While other things are changing they remain very much the same. It is a mistake to plant trees simply for one week of flower colour. The structure of the tree and the prolonged colour of the foliage must count for more than the blossom.

There are a number of things that go well with the silver of the willow. I have a purple berberis and a cotinus with greeny-purple leaves, *Cotinus coggygria* 'Foliis Purpureis', which goes well in front of the silver. Another plant that goes well with it is a blue veronica that has spikes of almost blue flowers with just a tinge of lavender and grows to about 1m (3ft) high. Then there are specks of really bright orange from the hips of a *Rosa moyesii*, which adds excitement.

Colour Control

If your garden is very small you do need to be more restrictive in the number of colours that you use. I always say to the gardener with a small garden that rather than have a number of small beds, it is better to have one large one because this gives scope for bigger effects, bigger groups. It is true that you cannot use the whole palette in one bed without something jarring. Although there is more of a case for restricting colours in the small garden, limiting the range of colour is often done as a defence mechanism by those who are not completely sure of what they are about, rather than through deliberate thought.

There is a lovely garden at Wakehurst Place, in West Sussex, a property now owned by the National Trust and leased to Kew Gardens.

The Henry Price Garden, planted in memory of the last private owner of Wakehurst, has flowers from all the colours of the spectrum but none is bright, they are all soft shades. It is wonderfully successful but I have sometimes suggested to the Assistant Curator, Tony Schilling, that now he has got the pastel shades out of his system he could try a combination of orange, yellow and red.

The private gardener who has experimented with one range of colours should also try something completely different, perhaps some of the more difficult combinations. If you have the facility for imagining how plants will look together it is a great asset. But it does not really matter if you haven't because you can try things out by holding one flower against another in the garden. The very fact that you can do this will tell you that they flower at the same time; when making your colour schemes it is important to ensure that the ingredients in your colour plan will flower simultaneously. Quite apart from that you can see whether the two flowers please you in other ways, for instance, whether you like their shapes together.

Almost certainly, you will make mistakes when combining colours, but that is not a reason to give up experimenting. Be as adventurous as you can with a full palette and with the wide range of exciting plants that are available to bring the full potential of colour into your garden.

The walled garden at Wakehurst Place in West Sussex, now owned by the National Trust and leased to Kew Gardens, is dedicated to the last private owner of the property, Sir Henry Price. The palette used excludes all the 'hard' colours, and silvery foliage and soft textures complement the pastel shades.

The Art of the Border

FRANCES PERRY

Several generations of gardeners have reason to thank Frances Perry for the straightforward common-sense advice she has given on garden matters over the years. She is, perhaps, best known as an authority on water plants – water gardening was the subject of her first book – but hardy herbaceous perennials are her great love. Her taste, however, is wonderfully catholic, as her own garden of about half an acre demonstrates. She has lived in the same village, Bull's Cross, Enfield, for most of her life and in her present home for nearly fifty years. Her early enthusiasm for plants and gardening was encouraged by E. A. Bowles, author of the *My Garden* series, whose home, Myddleton House, was nearby. Many of the plants she grows are associated with this fascinating and immensely knowledgeable plantsman.

Above all, Frances Perry is a practical person. She knows from her own experience and through observing other gardens that borders devoted exclusively to herbaceous perennials, although capable of producing some of the finest effects in the English tradition of gardening, require a scale of operation and a level of management that is beyond the resources of many gardeners. As she explains here, mixing shrubs and bulbs with perennials can be an equally rewarding form of gardening and one that is less demanding of time and space.

A bold colour scheme at Tintinhull House, Somerset, includes shrubs, roses, perennials – including half-hardy dahlias – and bulbs. With mixed plantings of this kind, it is easier to sustain interest in the garden than it is with borders of herbaceous perennials.

WHEN I ATTENDED MY FIRST Chelsea Flower Show in 1921, I was impressed not only by the extraordinary array of plants, flowers such as I had never seen in my life, but also by the people, the men in grey toppers and morning suits, the women with very large, flowery hats. This was the generation that had taken to heart the advice and example of William Robinson and Gertrude Jekyll, the most powerful influences on British gardening in the early twentieth century. For them hardy

herbaceous perennials were among the most important of ornamental plants and Miss Jekyll, in particular, made of their cultivation a refined art. In the country-house gardens that she designed so meticulously, often in collaboration with the architect Sir Edwin Lutyens, the herbaceous border became a major feature. Our idea of the herbaceous border remains very much Miss Jekyll's creation.

Herbaceous Borders

Although herbaceous borders are often thought of as typical features of British gardens, their history is much more recent than is sometimes supposed. In Phillip Miller's *Dictionary of Gardening*, published in 1724, there is a description of flower beds that are clearly the forerunners of the classic collections of herbaceous perennials: 'Gardeners are making borders along the sidewalks for their choicest plants', and 'where flowers are desired, there may be borders continued round the extent of the lawn, immediately before the plantation of shrubs, which if properly planted with hardy flowers to succeed each other will afford a more pleasing prospect.' But it was not until 1890 that the phrase 'herbaceous border' was first coined by George Nicolson, a curator of the Royal Botanic Gardens, Kew, and it was the great flood of plant introductions in the nineteenth century that made possible gardening with herbaceous perennials in the grand manner of the Edwardian country houses.

It was the First World War that marked the beginning of the end of country-house life on a lavish scale. But, even when I began my career in horticulture, there were many nurseries catering for a wealthy clientele who were growing large numbers of herbaceous perennials. (That first Chelsea Flower Show had given me the ambition to work in horticulture, although, according to my mother, my interest was established when, at the age of eighteen months, I fell head-first into a tub of liquid manure.)

Perry's Hardy Plant Farm, where I started after horticultural college,

The hardy perennials remain important border plants, even in mixed plantings. Among the most magnificant are the oriental poppies, Papaver orientale – they dominate this border – which were bred so successfully by Perry's Hardy Plant Farm, where Frances Perry began working after leaving horticultural college.

had an enviable reputation for the quality of its perennial plants. Amos Perry, a fifth-generation nurseryman, and his eldest son, Gerald, whom I eventually married, were enormously enthusiastic and knowledgeable about herbaceous perennials and both had very good eyes for spotting unusual and interesting plants. They very much influenced me in favour of hardy plants that can stand up and look after themselves. So, too, did the great gardener E.A. Bowles, whose home, Myddelton House, was just down the road from the hamlet where I was born and where I have spent most of my life. Bowles is probably now best remembered for his 'My Garden' trilogy, about his garden through the changing seasons. I was exceptionally lucky to be able to learn directly from someone who combined such a deep knowledge of plants with a character of charming eccentricity.

Growing these lovely herbaceous perennials separated from other plants in the garden was a splendid idea, a twin border at its peak creating a staggering effect, a tremendous kaleidoscope of breathtaking colour produced by plants from all over the world. But now there are fewer gardens where you can see herbaceous borders in the old style, although in public gardens, such as the Royal Botanic Gardens at Edinburgh or the Royal Horticultural Society's garden at Wisley, you can see token borders.

On the positive side, herbaceous borders give a sumptuous effect at the height of their season and it is a sound gardening policy to group together plants requiring similar care and attention. But their disadvantages cannot be denied. In a small garden you can't afford to devote a border to perennials that will be in character only from May to September each year. There may be a few plants that extend either end of this season but, in effect, herbaceous borders do not contribute to the beauty of the garden for half the year. That did not matter to the wealthy landowner with a large property cared for by trained gardeners and labourers. Country estates were often used only for short periods in the year and then the planting was geared to create a magnificent effect for the limited time of residence. For example, delphiniums and peonies probably featured as the dominant plants for a June display and Michaelmas daisies for late August and September.

Even if the house was used throughout the year, it did not matter that part of the garden was dead for some of the time. It was visited when at its peak and at other times the main interest of the garden would lie elsewhere. At lilac time, for instance, it might be the shrubbery, for woody plants, too, were treated as a group that was kept apart. It is easy to forget, however, how popular hardy ferns once were. As an underplanting, they were often combined with shrubs.

In some large gardens, perennials were treated almost as bedding plants. Gardeners maintained supplies of pot-grown plants, generally in greenhouses, and as a perennial disappeared or lost its beauty it was lifted and another put in its place. This technique was used by Thomas Hay (the father of my second husband), who was responsible for the central royal parks in London.

Queen Mary always liked to have delphiniums at Buckingham Palace, but there was one occasion when the beds had been cleared because it was thought that the ground was sick and a break would be beneficial.

Thomas Hay got to hear of the Queen's displeasure and, remembering that he had a greenhouse area with a lot of delphiniums in pots just coming into flower, got the area replanted very early in the morning. The Queen could not believe her eyes. King George V sent for Thomas Hay and said, offering him a sherry and a cigar, 'I want to thank you for what you did with the delphiniums. It saved me a lot of bother – a lot of bother.'

Mixed borders

At its best, the herbaceous border is remarkably beautiful, but, as it is dead for certain periods, it depends for its success partly on being set in a large garden, so that the gardener need not rely on it to perform throughout the year, and partly on skilled planning and maintenance. It has suffered, therefore, from two consistent trends in gardening. The most obvious is that many gardens are smaller due to infilling and most houses being built on smaller plots. So we have had to find ways of gardening that give us a good range of seasonal interest within a small area. When help is needed, there is also the difficulty of finding people who are skilled. And, because our lives seem to be so busy, this can mean finding a style of gardening that does not involve time-consuming maintenance.

These developments are enough to explain the decline of the herbaceous border in favour of mixed planting, in which herbaceous perennials are combined with shrubs and bulbs, even annuals. Today we cannot afford to be purists; mixed borders are simply an

Mixed borders are long-term garden features; their planning and preparation should not be rushed. Although a sunny sheltered position with well-drained loamy soil is ideal, there are plants for almost all conditions.

acknowledgement of the facts of life. And, if we are quite truthful, this method of prolonging the season and reducing maintenance is a more natural way of growing plants; in nature herbaceous perennials do not grow as a group apart.

Preparing and planning

There are some disadvantages in growing perennials and bulbs mixed with shrubs but most can be overcome by good preparation of the ground, careful planning and feeding. The ideal site for a mixed border is a sunny, sheltered position with well-drained loamy soil. In a small garden, however, there is very often little choice about where a border is going to be. Fortunately, such a wide range of plants is available that an appropriate selection can be made whatever the particular conditions – dry or moist, acid or limy, sunny or shady.

Having chosen the site for your border, do not rush in to planting before you have got the preliminary work done. This border will serve you for a long time satisfactorily only if you take trouble at the outset. Cleanliness of the ground is very important. If you have got perennial weeds, you must begin by getting rid of them, otherwise they will be a never-ending source of trouble. With weeds such as ground elder you may need to use chemical weedkillers; these are safe provided you follow the manufacturer's instructions exactly.

Before the development of chemical controls, other methods had to be used. I remember Amos Perry getting rid of established ground elder by covering the weed with a good layer of straw. (Ground elder likes to have its roots near the surface.) In autumn the straw was raked off, the ground elder and its roots coming away with it. The process had to be repeated a second year but the nursery was cleared of the weed. In my own garden we got rid of it by planting Jerusalem artichokes. It was during war-time and we were keeping rabbits. They loved the green tops, so we kept pinching these out and feeding them to the rabbits. The artichokes built up such a dense canopy that the ground elder was starved out.

Soil improvement Once the ground is clear of perennial weeds it should be well dug, but only if the soil is in a fit state to be worked. For instance, the soil should not be so wet that it crumbles. Most gardeners find that the best time to prepare a bed is in autumn. If you have the strength and energy to double-dig, working the ground to a depth of two spits, that is fine but I don't know many people who do it today. My own garden hasn't been double-dug for ages, though we could do it because we are on light soil. On a heavy clay you can often do more harm than good by double-digging. I remember going as an advisor to a garden on really awful clay soil where the owner had planted apple-trees, which had suddenly started dying. Before planting he had double-dug the area and the effect had been to create a pond under the ground. The apple-trees were dying because their roots were reaching the water. The smell was really appalling.

That is rather an exceptional case but remember that only bog and water plants are happy in water-logged conditions. Most gardens are reasonably well drained but if there is a danger of water standing after heavy rain or during the winter, improve the drainage. To improve thin, dry soils, incorporate moisture-retentive organic material, such as well-rotted compost. Do not make the mistake of thinking that because an area is shady it will be moist. Very often these areas are quite dry – they are in rain shadow as well as sun shadow – presenting the gardener with rather difficult conditions. By incorporating moisture-retentive material you will increase the range of plants that can be grown satisfactorily. Whatever the soil, work in plenty of organic matter. Once the border is planted, there will not be a comparable opportunity to improve the soil's texture and fertility.

The right background

Before drawing up the planting scheme decide what kind of background you want. You might simply use tall shrubs, or there may be an existing hedge, fence or wall. The living green architecture of hedges shows off flowers to good advantage but also presents some problems. Many hedge plants – privet and yew are the most notorious in this respect – feed greedily from the beds and they also need periodic trimming. If possible, separate the border from the hedge by a path; it will make access for clipping much easier and the competition for nutrients will be less direct. Walls and fences do not rob plants of food and will support climbers at the back of the border. A mellow wall makes a lovely background but having one built has become prohibitively expensive. It is, of course, possible to have a border that is viewed from front and back. The great nurseryman Alan Bloom has popularized island beds for perennials, a method of growing them that can be adapted for mixed borders. Many plants in island beds do not require staking, although they would in a border in front of a wall or ledge.

Planting schemes

It is tempting to think that haphazard planting will produce a delightfully natural effect and there are a few very talented gardeners who have a knack for apparently random planting that is marvellously effective, but most of us need to be more methodical. By far the best method of planning a border is to draw it to scale on a large sheet of paper and to fit on to it a jigsaw puzzle of shrubs and groups of plants, taking into account such factors as height, spread, flowering season and colour. This allows you to think through the implications of your scheme and avoid errors that might be troublesome to put right.

It is important to have an idea of the height plants are going to reach. You don't want a giant in the front row, particularly if you have short things behind. When a border will be looked at from only one side, the tallest subjects should be kept to the back but a strictly stepped arrangement would look very forced. You could use shrubs to create informal bays, a device that, with a long border flanking a path, creates an element of mystery. To avoid too rigid an arrangement, try bringing forward a tall, airy plant, such as a campanula or thalictrum. A border that is looked at from more than one side is more difficult to plan but the aim should be to have the tallest plants grouped centrally.

To the inexperienced gardener, spread is often much more problematic than height. Plants must be given sufficient space to allow for full development but most perennials take two years to reach maturity and

shrubs longer still. Even experienced gardeners tend to plant too thickly to avoid gaps and bare patches in the first season. It is probably a cheaper and better policy to use annuals and bulbs to fill gaps in the first year rather than to overplant with expensive shrubs and perennials. Until a body of personal experience has been built up, the gardener has to depend on observation of plants in other gardens and the information available in nurserymen's catalogues. From the outset, plant perennials in groups. An acanthus or a peony may be large enough to make a striking effect as a single specimen but, as a general rule, groupings of three, five or seven are to be preferred, making a bold splash of colour or a handsome mass of foliage.

The height to which plants will grow is an important factor to take into account when drawing up a planting scheme. Shrubs, of course, will take several years to reach maturity.

To make the most of the all-purpose border's prolonged display, the gardener must plan to take advantage of both flower and foliage seasons. It is not simply a matter of having a display from the first winter-flowering shrubs and bulbs until the dying leaves of autumn but also of blending colours harmoniously. Some believe that colours in the garden never clash but they certainly can. Brilliant scarlet, orange and petunia pink, for example, make a shrieking confusion of colour if mixed closely together. Use foliage to separate difficult tones and combine others to create a brilliant effect or a more subtle harmony.

Also take account of the idiosyncracies of individual plants. Do not thoughtlessly combine moisture-loving plants, such as monarda and phlox, with others that prefer free-draining conditions, like catmint; or acid-lovers, such as rhododendrons, with lime-lovers, such as bearded irises. It helps, too, if you know the snags associated with particular plants. For instance, something like the oriental poppy that is untidy after flowering is not a plant for the front of a border. It needs to be set back so that a late-season plant can be grown in front of it to hide the unsightly way its foliage dies down at the end of its active period.

71

As a final point I would recommend marking on your plan those perennials that need frequent division. There will be some that you can leave for years. Acanthus, for example, is one that you would be well advised to leave completely alone or else you will get it all over the border; in my garden it is all mixed up with tree peonies. But others, like the bearded irises and the rubellum chrysanthemums, need frequent division to maintain a good display. Recognizing this at the planning stage can be very helpful.

Some Desirable Plants

So many good plants are suitable for mixed borders that all I will do here is to indicate the qualities and virtues that I look out for when making my own choice.

Colour for winter

The shrubs that help us through the dullest part of the year, from the beginning to the end of winter, are to my way of thinking particularly valuable. During these months there are very few herbaceous plants to give the garden a lift so it is not surprising that the winter-flowering heathers have become so popular. They are persistent, they never get too tall, they do not seem to mind a bit of snow and there are kinds that will tolerate most soils, even those that are limey. I would be very sorry not to have varieties of *Erica carnea* such as 'King George', a good crimson, 'Springwood White' and 'Pink Spangles', or forms of the hybrid *E. × darleyensis* such as the white 'Silberschmelze'. Some forms have very attractively coloured foliage and most will do well in light shade as well as full sun, although their flowering will be better in an open position.

Among the taller, winter-flowering shrubs, the viburnums are particularly good. We have a hedge of *V. farreri*, which must go back to the 1920s and was raised from seed that the collector, Reginald Farrer, sent back to E.A. Bowles. It grows to about 4m (12ft) and carries compact heads of fragrant flowers from October to April, as does another species, *V. grandiflorum*, and *V. × bodnantense*, a hybrid between these two. These three are all deciduous but laurustinus (*V. tinus*) is an evergreen winter-flowering species with flat heads of white flowers that are pink in the bud. Other good winter-flowering shrubs include the mezereon (*Daphne mezereum*), the winter-flowering jasmine (*Jasminum nudiflorum*) and the witch hazels (*Hamamelis* species and cultivars).

Berrying plants are also very useful in winter. I am particularly attached to the skimmias, which don't grow much more than 1.2m (4ft) tall and can be smothered in scarlet berries for most of the year. *S. japonica* is one where you have to have a male as a pollinator for the females but another species, *S. reevesiana*, is hermaphrodite so only one plant is needed. It is astonishing that a plant can be colourful for so long. Last year I had one in the garden that was covered in berries for fourteen months.

The cotoneasters are also attractive, berrying shrubs that give a good account of themselves in winter. The best known is probably the deciduous *C. horizontalis*, with its distinctive herring-bone branches. It makes a very striking wall shrub but tends to lose its berries earlier than the evergreen *C. conspicuus* and the semi-evergreen *C.* × *watereri*.

Grey-leaved shrubs

This is another very useful group; these shrubs do best in full sun and in well-drained soil, their greyness improving in a hot summer. They are particularly effective in toning down bright flower colour, often making it possible to combine in the same border colours that might otherwise seem antagonistic. *Senecio* 'Sunshine' is a very reliable plant with leaves beautifully outlined in grey but there are many other shrubby and sub-shrubby plants, including artemisias, ballotas and santolinas, that are interesting for their texture as well as their colour. Some grey-leaved plants are also highly aromatic; two that are very particularly nice to have in the garden to touch and to smell are lavender and rosemary.

Classic flowering shrubs

Whatever the merits of other shrubs, those that continue to be most lavishly used in mixed borders are the classic flowering shrubs, such as rhododendrons, philadelphus and roses. They are all plants of excellent qualities (some having the great merit of being exquisitely fragrant) but the repeat-flowering roses have the great advantage of giving a long season of colour. Some floribundas – or cluster-flowered bush roses, as

A skilful mixture of plants, including geraniums, lavender and large shrubs, gives weight to this planting of roses at Polesden Lacey in Surrey.

they are now called – flower almost continuously over a very long period. 'Iceberg', for instance, will often still be in flower almost up until Christmas. If you put roses into a mixed border there are two things to take into account right from the start. Roses are attacked by diseases and pests and therefore need to be sprayed, and they also need to be pruned. To avoid damaging other plants by clambering to reach the roses or by fall-out from your spray, position them where they are easily accessible.

Climbers

If you have a good wall or fence at the back of the border, climbing roses can make a spectacular background. We have found that *Clematis* × *jackmanii* goes particularly well with some of the climbers. It can be cut right back in autumn or winter and when the new shoots come away in spring and early summer, make sure they have got a start and away they will go to give a magnificent combination of red roses and blue clematis.

There are other good climbers for a sunny wall. The passion flower (*Passiflora caerulea*) produces masses of its curious flowers in mid-summer and in a good year may even bear orange-red, oval berries. The solanums are also good wall plants. The family resemblance to the potato shows in the clusters of flowers. The most spectacular is *S. crispum*, which can grow to a height of 4.5m (15ft) and has rich blue flowers but it is not quite as hardy as *S. jasminoides*, a species with slate-blue flowers, although there is also a good white form. Another often tender plant for a warm sheltered wall is the showy, yellow-flowered *Fremontodendron californicum*, which will flower on and off all summer. But if you are looking for hardier plants it is difficult to beat the honeysuckles, which flower better in a sunny position than in shade. The best for scent is *Lonicera periclymenum* and its selected forms but others, such as the red-flowered *L.* × *brownii*, are more colourful.

Some climbing plants will give you a very good display on a shaded wall. One of the best is the self-clinging, deciduous *Hydrangea petiolaris*. A mature plant can reach a height of 15m (50ft) but it is not difficult to keep it in check with pruning. A quieter plant is *Akebia quinata*, which has hand-shaped leaves and purple fragrant flowers. Unfortunately, in our garden we only occasionally get its strange, sausage-like fruits. Remember, too, that there are good foliage plants for shady walls, among them parthenocissus and many ivies (*Hedera*), some of which have attractively variegated foliage.

Bulbs

These must certainly be the most useful plants for adding colour to the border at either end of the main season. In addition to the obvious hyacinths, narcissi and tulips there are many small bulbs, some of which come into flower in the dead of winter. There are snowdrops (*Galanthus* species and cultivars), of course, but also winter aconites (*Eranthis hyemalis*) and species crocuses such as the lovely forms of *C. chrysanthus*. Mr Bowles taught me that these are all bulbs that are best lifted and moved during the growing season. It is something he discovered when segregating selected forms. You would hear him say,

'That's a good crocus,' and he would dig it up and put it somewhere else. He named many of the forms we still grow. Other dwarf bulbs to try for early spring are chionodoxas, grape hyacinths (*Muscari*), ipheions, dwarf irises, scillas and perhaps some of the dwarf narcissi, such as *N. bulbocodium*.

At the other end of the season, there are more crocuses, particularly forms of *C. speciosus*, the splendid globular flowers of colchicums and cyclamen. The best known of these is the autumn-flowering *C. hederifolium*, a plant that you can leave to look after itself for years but which is exquisite in flower and very attractive in leaf. Mr Bowles used to say that no two leaves are alike and he would offer five shillings to anyone who could find two the same.

Of the summer bulbs, lilies are in a class of their own. There are now hundreds, even thousands, of cultivated varieties to chose from, many of sumptuous form and brilliant colouring. However, there are few to match the regal lily (*Lilium regale*) for reliability and loveliness. It is one of the many plants of superior quality we owe to E.H. Wilson, 'Chinese Wilson', who discovered it near the border of China and Tibet in 1904.

Small bulbs can pose a slight problem of organization in mixed borders; they are easily dispersed when the ground is being forked over. But that is not a problem with what I call the volunteers. There are a number of plants that self-seed freely and are a delight to have in a border, giving an effect that you could never achieve by deliberate planting. The Welsh poppy (*Meconopsis cambrica*) is a case in point. I wouldn't be without it, although I sometimes get wild when I get too many among other good plants. Normally yellow and orange, in our garden we have had the great good fortune to turn up a few scarlets. Other off-beat plants which we wouldn't be without are the variegated forms of honesty (*Lunaria annua*). They flower just after the daffodils, when you haven't got much else. Once they have finished flowering, unless you want to keep them for the seedpods or a few for seed, you can pull them up. They are always better plants when they volunteer to come up themselves. You can't fool with them; you must leave them alone and then you will get good plants. *Helleborus corsicus*, a handsome species with green flowers in winter, is another plant that has got to sow itself where it wants to. The poached egg flower (*Limnanthes douglasii*), an annual, is not such a fussy plant but it is a lovely thing to have self-seeding and will keep itself going quite happily in the border.

Annuals and bedding plants
In my estimation, these do not normally feature in the top rank of ornamentals. However, on occasions they can be very useful in mixed borders. For example, the winter-flowering pansies can give a good show of colour at the bleakest time of the year and, particularly in the early stages of a border, clumps of annuals can fill awkward gaps.

Hardy herbaceous plants
I began by referring to the traditional herbaceous border and I have to admit my preference for the hardy herbaceous plants that used to be grown in them. I would certainly want them to feature prominently in my mixed borders. The choice is so wide that it is impossible to make a

selection that would be helpful to other gardeners. I can only say that my favourites include many of those with blue flowers. I love all the salvias, from the ordinary culinary sage to beauties like the somewhat tender *S. patens*, which has flowers of intense deep blue. And then, of course, there are delphiniums, the blue blood of the border. They are a bit of trouble because they have to be staked, the shoots may have to be thinned and they have to be watched early in the year to see that slugs don't get them. But they are well worth the effort. I would not want to be without blue campanulas or blue irises, such as the grassy-leaved sibirica types. I would welcome, too, blue-flowered perennials such as aconitum, baptisias, echinops, phlox and scabious. But you can see that this is very much a personal taste. Other gardeners will have a preference for the splendid golds and russets of achilleas, coreopsis, heleniums and rudbeckias or the reds and pinks of mallows, peonies and oriental poppies. What is certain is that there is no dearth of plants to choose from and that through the activities of bodies such as The Hardy Plant Society, many very good perennials that might have been forgotten have regained an enthusiastic following.

Maintenance

A mixed border is less time-consuming to maintain than a herbaceous border but from time to time shrubs will need pruning and most perennials will need to be divided every three years or so if they are not to deteriorate. In the growing season some of the finest perennials need staking; if they are not supported, the stems can be bent or snapped by heavy rain and strong winds. All supports should be put in while growth is still quite short because damage cannot be undone. Twiggy peasticks are versatile and unobtrusive supports but they are not easy to come by; for many gardeners the only suitable alternative will be metal ring supports. Tall-growing plants, including delphiniums and lilies, need to be tied to individual canes. Use a tie that does not shout out from the border. Dead-heading will prevent plants wasting energy in seed production and will also help to keep the garden looking neat and tidy. Weeding is a chore that can never be neglected but the use of a good mulch of well-rotted organic matter will discourage weeds, keep the ground moist and return fertility to the soil. Horse manure and other animal manures are no longer readily available – and when they are they can be expensive – so your own compost heap is very important to the garden. Provided that you put on a good organic mulch, you will not need to use a lot of chemical fertilizer but a spring feed will be beneficial and perhaps a dressing of bonemeal in autumn.

The Long Border at Great Dixter in East Sussex is a very fine example of mixed planting in which staged climaxes follow one another throughout the whole year.

I hope that listing the jobs to be done won't discourage gardeners from making the most of their borders. We are very fortunate in Britain in still having many magnificent gardens open to the public, which can serve as a source of inspiration even when you are gardening on a small suburban scale. It is a matter of being observant and noting successful plant associations, colour schemes that could be translated into your own small border, and successful ways of treating difficult areas. If you are observant, there is a great wealth of professional expertise and traditional knowledge on which to draw.

Foliage, Form and Colour

Long before meeting Penelope Hobhouse, I had come to know of her knowledge and love of plants and gardens through the books that have made her one of the most widely read of modern gardening writers. *A Book of Gardening* fascinated me particularly, as it brings together the experience of many of those responsible for some of the finest gardens in Britain – those that are owned by the National Trust. It is easy to think that the gardens attached to great houses hold no lessons for the ordinary gardener. But, as Penelope Hobhouse herself found at Tintinhull House in Somerset when she was just starting out on her career as a gardener, one can always learn from a garden where plants have been used well. Mrs Reiss, who developed the garden at Tintinhull and who gave it to the National Trust, made lavish use of foliage for subtle as well as for showy effects. By a happy quirk of fate, Penelope Hobhouse and her husband, Professor John Mallins, now look after the garden at Tintinhull.

It was at Tintinhull that I interrupted Penelope Hobhouse's busy schedule as a writer, garden planning consultant, lecturer and practical gardener for a long discussion about the use of foliage in the garden. I had much to learn, but we began in agreement that there is still room in most gardens for more adventurous use of plants for their leaves rather than solely for their flowers.

MANY GARDENERS must start as I did, keen to make something beautiful with plants but without having been particularly interested in them as a child and without having much experience of growing them. I suppose that in my very first ideas of garden-making I concentrated on flowers. This is the starting point for many gardeners and some indeed never really progress beyond it. After all, they seem the obvious constituents of a garden, wonderfully varied in shape and colour, sometimes deliciously scented and, if chosen with discrimination, they give a display in your garden throughout the year.

Looking back now at my first vision of the garden I wanted, I can appreciate how blind I was, how I looked at the countryside, at plants and at trees simply as living wallpaper without in any way penetrating to the detail. If I had been more observant, I would have recognized from the beginning the importance of foliage in making a garden of sustained interest – at Tintinhull, as you will see, the foliage is the crucial element in creating the tight, formal feel that is a key factor in the overall effect.

A large holm oak (Quercus ilex) dominates this view of Tintinhull House, a property in Somerset now owned by the National Trust, where the use of foliage plants by Mrs Reiss, the previous owner, made such an impression on Penelope Hobhouse at an early stage in her gardening career. She and her husband are now responsible for the upkeep of the garden. The holm oak is one of the most majestic evergreen trees that can be grown in Britain.

Early Impressions

One of the most important early experiences that opened my eyes to the value of foliage was a visit I made to Tintinhull House when I was twenty-five, married with two small children and faced with the job of making a garden of my own. It still strikes me as a very curious turn of events that in 1980, my husband and I should become responsible for the day-to-day running of the garden, which since 1954 has been owned by the National Trust.

I was completely bowled over by my first visit. It was an emotional and aesthetic experience beyond all my expectations and one that made me aware for the first time that gardening was an art form. What impressed me more than anything else were the colour schemes. Mrs Reiss, who made the garden as it is and lived here from 1933 until her death in 1962, had created within a framework of seperate hedged compartments a series of quite different effects using carefully chosen associations of flowers and foliage.

One of her most famous schemes and one that made an enormous impression on me at that time was a border featuring gold and purple foliage. She had used a golden cornus (*Cornus alba* 'Spaethii'), a purple-leaved prunus (*Prunus cerasifera* 'Pissardii') and different forms of purple-leaved berberis. With these she had combined crimson roses and very bright blue veronica. There was a lot of blue pigment running through the flowers and the purple leaves but what really hit me was the contrast between the purple and gold foliage. This bold statement made me understand that it was possible to plan colour effects and to garden imaginatively without relying exclusively on flowers.

Since living at Tintinhull we have found the purple and gold border almost too much of a good thing. We have introduced several plants to soften the harsh contrast: two *Berberis* with grey foliage, *B. temolaica* and *B. dictyyophylla* 'Approximata', and *Viburnum sargentiri* 'Oneida'. The more mature you become as a gardener the more subtle are the effects you want but the toning down of the gold and purple border has not destroyed its usefulness to the public as a teaching border.

Unifying Themes

One other characteristic of the garden at Tintinhull that I noticed on my first visit was the way plant shapes and foliage colour were repeated throughout the garden. There would be a great group of *Senecio* 'Sunshine', which you would meet again when you moved on to another compartment.

I am not sure to what extent the wonderful feeling of the garden being all linked together was a planned effect. Mrs Reiss wasn't really a plantswoman and often she didn't have access to a lot of new plants. She was more interested in specific effects and she did not mind using the same plant in different situations to get the result that she wanted. She used a purple-leaved *Cotinus* a great deal, now I would say too much. But the impact of this garden held together with foliage colour and shapes made a great impression on me and had a strong influence on my own gardening.

Architectural Foliage

At Tintinhull the use of foliage was taken a stage further. The tight formal design, which I found so exciting, was created by yew hedges and axial paths flanked by pairs of box bushes clipped into domes. Here was foliage transformed by shaping into living architecture.

In Italy, which I began to visit at about the time I first came to Tintinhull, I discovered the sober beauty of Renaissance gardens. Very often, these contained no bright colour to distract from the play of light on the greens and greys of box and yew, Italian cypresses and *Quercus ilex*, and occasionally ancient stonework. The dignity and restraint of

This collection of variegated foliage and blue-green leaves at Tintinhull House demonstrates the very rich and subtle effects that can be achieved without flower colour. *Melianthus major*, the jagged-leaved perennial behind *Ruta graveolens* 'Jackman's Blue', is a slightly tender South African species but among the finest foliage plants that can be grown outdoors in the milder parts of Britain.

those Italian gardens is much more extreme than you find in British gardens such as Sissinghurst Castle or Hidcote Manor, in both of which formal hedging plays such an important role.

In the case of Hidcote, for example, not only do the hedges provide a background to an exceptionally rich collection of plants but also they are made of different materials. As well as planting hedges of box and yew, Major Lawrence Johnston, who created the garden, planted others of beech, holly, hornbeam and lime, and even some that are tapestries, mixtures of more than one kind of plant.

The Renaissance gardens of Italy reinforced what I had learned from Tintinhull about the architectural use of foliage but, so powerful was the impression they made on me, that I sometimes felt that shades of green and grey were quite enough in a garden.

Texture, Size and Shape

It was at Tintinhull that I first learned about the use of leaf colour and the importance of foliage in forming the structure of a garden and in giving a background to what might be a fleeting display of flowers. What I have also come to value in foliage – its wonderfully varied textures and the fascinating range of size and shape – I first appreciated with real excitement at Abbotsbury, near the Devon coast. When I first knew this magnificent collection of sub-tropical plants (started about

1815 by the Lord Ilchester of the day) it was romantically overgrown, a glorious mixture of palms, plants with very large and glossy leaves, dark greens and, in sharp contrast, jagged, small-leaved and grey plants from Australasia that were capable of standing up to hot dry conditions.

Abbotsbury was certainly one of the gardens that fired me with the passion of the collector. For instance, I wanted to get hold of every evergreen shrub that I could grow. Their Latin names enthralled me and were part of the spell. I quickly learned, however, that growing plants – foliage plants as well as flowering ones – in a way that is aesthetically satisfying does not follow automatically from successful and extensive collecting.

I love going to look at the wonderful plantsmen's gardens in Cornwall, or at the woodland gardens in Sussex created by the Loder family. Nonetheless, it is always an enormous relief when I find that they have been gardened not only with the enthusiasm of the collector but also with good taste, so that the plants are presented in a setting that has form and shape. The gardener has to find a balance between the pull of the collector and the pull of the designer. Reconciling these two opposing forces is one of the great themes of the British tradition of gardening and should not be neglected even when the garden is on a very modest scale.

Evergreen Trees and Shrubs

Evergreen trees and shrubs would still be the plants with which I would start a collection and box (*Buxus sempervirens*) and yew (*Taxus baccata*), despite their familiarity, would feature in the first rank. As hedging plants they are invaluable, making dense even-textured surfaces that are relatively easy to maintain. Clipped specimens arranged in groups – for example, paired rows flanking a path – can be used in conjunction with hedges and walls to define the structure of a garden and to give it a formal rhythm.

The seasonal changes of deciduous trees are quite obvious, but it is often forgotten that evergreens change in colour and texture throughout the year. In spring, box and yew both have lovely, soft, pale growth which forms a tapestry with the darker foliage beneath. By July you are back to the wonderfully solid, dark green shapes that hold the garden together through the year.

Hollies, again very familiar plants, are the sort of thing I like a lot. Gertrude Jekyll and William Robinson both made the point that in a country garden you should use native plants towards the perimeter and keep exotics closer to the house. Hollies and junipers were the kind of plants Miss Jekyll used in her own garden to avoid the jarring of the senses at the point where garden and countryside meet.

In gardening, however, you are always contradicting the rules you lay down. The Robinsonian wild garden is, after all, a wonderful mixture of native and exotic plants. Nonetheless, there is a rightness in the way plants are put together and the holly is certainly one that looks at home in the English landscape.

I would love to make a collection of hollies, for the sake of their beautifully glossy green leaves. I would not include a variegated one,

for they remind me too much of a Victorian shrubbery. Hollies are not plants to make a mistake with because they are very slow growing and once they are there you feel that you can't change them. I found this at Hadspen House, where I restored the Edwardian garden. A lot of the hedgehog holly (*I. aquifolium* 'Ferox') had been planted under dark yews. They made spots of colour a long way off and seemed fussy.

My choice for a perfectly ordinary hedging holly would nearly always be *I. aquifolium* 'J.C. van Tol', which has wonderfully lustrous leaves and no spines. A less common species that I like very much is *I. cornuta*, the leaves of which are almost stemless, curiously rectangular and only lightly spined.

Scale and Form
The foliage of the holm oak (*Quercus ilex*), one of the most majestic evergreen trees that can be grown in Britain, makes a very different impact to that of holly. From the main bedroom at Tintinhull the sky is framed by two large holm oaks at the bottom of the garden. These are a constant reminder to me of how different the densities and weights of evergreens can be and how much their qualities change according to the light in which they are seen. The leathery leaves of the holm oak are shiny dark green on the upper surface and downy grey on the underside. This is not a tree for the very coldest parts of the country, nor is it suitable in most circumstances for the small or even moderately

The main axis at Tintinhull House is flanked by pairs of clipped box, the symmetrical arrangement emphasizing the formality of the garden. Box and yew are the most valuable foliage plants to use as architectural elements in the garden.

sized garden. However, it does respond well to clipping. At Hatfield House in Hertfordshire round-headed standards on clean stems about 1.8m (6ft) high have been used to create a double avenue. A pair, growing in huge Versailles tubs, could flank a main door.

Conifers

When people want a majestic tree they are very often tempted to plant a conifer. I must admit I am not tremendously interested in this group of plants. The English go mad about wellingtonias (*Sequoiadendron giganteum*) but a single one looks absolutely absurd; they only look right when forming part of a stand. A cedar in the right place can look lovely but I particularly dislike the grey-leaved *Cedrus atlantica* 'Glauca', which, I am afraid, you see all too often. Blue-grey leaves can be wonderful at eye level but when they belong to a large specimen tree they are too dominant in the landscape.

At the other end of the scale there is an almost frenzied planting of small conifers and heathers, not a kind of gardening that I like. Although all these plants have texture, there is not enough contrast so that, despite all the little verticals of conifers, no real sense of form is created.

There is a dead quality to the texture of quite a number of conifers, including forms of *Chamaecyparis lawsoniana* and × *Cupressocyparis leylandii*, the Lawson and Leyland cypresses, which are so often planted like electric lamp posts in front gardens. The deciduous swamp cypress (*Taxodium distichum*) is another matter. The foliage is a lovely, glowing fresh green in summer and in autumn turns a glorious browny orange. The other outstanding deciduous conifer is the maidenhair tree (*Ginkgo biloba*). The fan shape of the undivided leaves is itself unusual; and in autumn they turn clear yellow.

Conifers are very often chosen as screening plants or wind breaks. At Tresco, where they used *Pinus radiata* and *Cupressus macrocarpa*, they have found that some of the old trees ought to have been replaced long ago. When they go over on that very thin soil and the wind gets in, a lot of damage can be done. In new planting they are replacing *Pinus radiata* with the bishop's pine (*Pinus muricata*).

In many situations, I would not plant a straight line of conifers. If I am planting to hide a tennis court, for example, rather than put in rows of conifers that would accentuate the shape, I would prefer to take a bit more land and plant a grove of something like Portugal laurel (*Prunus lusitanica*). The bushy evergreen growth makes a good wind filter and, with a free planting, you can disguise the outline of the court.

Choice Evergreens

There are many choice evergreen shrubs that I would like to have: *Azara microphylla*, with shiny leaves and a curiously flattened way of growing, the holly-like *Itea ilicifolia*, and some of the rather tender pittosporums (in the relatively cold garden at Tintinhull we only grow *P. tobira*) would all count among them. But there are two plants at least that I would put before all these. The Mexican orange (*Choisya ternata*) must come close to being my favourite shrub. It is wonderful against stone or brickwork, can be used just as effectively in formal as in informal planting and its

Good foliage plants, including handsome evergreens such as Fatsia japonica, make a sheltered private enclosure at one end of a small garden.

glossy, aromatic leaves are never boring. It also has deliciously fragrant white flowers in spring.

Escallonia 'Iveyi' is almost equally desirable but, sadly, these last three winters have proved that this plant is not hardy. Fortunately, if damaged by frost, it can be cut back to old wood and new shoots will come away. Best planted against a sunny wall, this variety has very good glossy leaves and panicles of white flowers in late summer, a very useful time of the year to have a shrub flowering.

Variations on Green

It is worth remembering the flower-like colour effect that some foliage gives at certain times of the year. The finest display of young red foliage is given by cultivars and hybrids of *Pieris*. These acid-loving shrubs are best in woodland conditions; a light canopy may protect them from spring frosts that can damage young growth. The hybrid *P.* 'Forest Flame' produces the most startlingly brilliant colour but cultivars such as *P. formosa forrestii* 'Wakehurst' are almost as vivid.

The photinias, too, have striking copper-red foliage in spring. *Pieris.* x *fraseri* 'Birmingham' and 'Red Robin' both have glossy, dark green mature leaves but the young growth is bronzy and bright red in colour respectively.

Another of my favourite plants marks a shift away in another direction from the main range of greens. The shrubby hare's ear (*Bupleurum fruticosum*) is an exceptionally beautiful Mediterranean plant with glaucous foliage, perhaps one should say almost glaucous foliage, for one really sees it as green. However, it goes perfectly with grey foliage, combining particularly well with another of my favourites, *Artemisia* 'Powis Castle'.

We ought to be able to read from leaves a great deal about the conditions in which plants grow naturally. Most of the plants with grey and silvery foliage thrive in full sun and tolerate rather dry conditions. Their greyness is caused by a layer of small hairs, in some cases forming a dense felt, on the surface of the leaf. In most cases, too much shade and growing conditions that are too rich or too moist will produce an untypical plant and may even lead to its death.

I passed through a phase of having a great passion for *Phlomis italica*, which has stems and leaves that are very hairy and white, and a pale pink flower. I have come to recognize that it can be excessively woody and straggly and have transferred my loyalty to two other species. *Phlomis anatolica* is a relatively new introduction with bigger and less silvery leaves than those of *P.italica*. The grey rounded bush of *P. chrysophylla* has a slightly greenish gold tinge. Both plants look very good with shrub roses but the rich feeding that roses need is not for them.

Deciduous Shrubs and Trees

Among deciduous shrubs and trees there are some excellent grey-leaved plants. The weeping pear (*Pyrus salicifolia* 'Pendula') is very good, but is becoming a suburban commonplace. Another pear that makes a small tree or large shrub is *P. elaeagrifolia*, which, as its name suggests, is like a grey-leaved elaeagnus. The Russian olive (*Elaeagnus angustifolia*), especially the form 'Caspica', should itself be much better known. Of pendulous habit, with soft grey, semi-evergreen leaves, it bears scented yellow flowers.

Gardeners rarely think of roses as foliage plants but I find *Rosa glauca* almost indispensable. It has clear pink flowers but its grey leaves, red-tinged stems and bright red fruits that make it really worth growing.

With some other roses, the quality of their foliage is an additional reason for growing them. In the case of the albas 'Maxima' and 'Celestial' the blue-grey foliage perfectly compliments the flowers. *Rosa soulieana* has lovely pale-grey foliage, too. The ferny foliage of others is very appealing, as is the case with *R. moyesii* and 'Canary Bird'. The bronze foliage of some such as 'Rosemary Rose' and 'Nathalie Nypels'

The quality of rose foliage is often neglected. In spring the new tender growth can be flushed soft red. A rose that is worth growing just for its blue-green leaves is *R. glauca* (formerly *R. rubrifolia*), which here complements the mauve of a large-flowered clematis, 'Victoria'. The flowers of *R. glauca* give a short season of interest but there are fine hips in late summer.

can also be exploited. Perhaps one of the most extraordinary roses is R. *omeiensis*, its chief ornamental attribute being the wonderful red translucence of its thorns.

Among the willows (*Salix*) are many species and cultivars with attractive foliage in shades of grey. You can get some idea of the range from the collection at Knightshayes Court in Devon. I have to admit that if I were allowed only one willow it would not be grey-leaved. I would choose *S. sachalinensis* 'Sekka', which has slender, pointed ever-green leaves. At Tintinhull we do grow a silvery willow, *S. helvetica*, but on standards clipped into a ball shape.

On a different scale and with a quite different effect I have used the ball shapes of another deciduous tree, the mop-headed robinia (*R. pseudocacacia* 'Inermis'). In a French garden with a border about 91m (100yd) long backed by a yew hedge I have used a row of about six to 'peg down' the border so that it doesn't seem to float.

Assertive Foliage

Grey is not difficult to handle but some of the stronger colours that you get in foliage certainly are. I have already mentioned the powerful impression made on me by the gold and purple border at Tintinhull. Now, I would be very cautious about planting large trees and shrubs with such assertive colour. Purple beech (*Fagus sylvatica* 'Riversii') more often than not clogs up a landscape and towards the end of summer the foliage becomes really heavy and coarse. I am advising on a garden that was landscaped by Humphry Repton in 1793. A feature of it is a hanging wood of purple-leaved beech, which was almost certainly not planted by him. It is the sort of colour that he never introduced and in a Repton landscape it is quite wrong but you couldn't take out a dozen fantastically good trees and they are so good that I have almost come to like them massed together.

In a park, golden leaves look out of place but there are golden-leaved shrubs that can be very effective in the garden. I am rather nervous of the golden-leaved elder, *Sambucus racemosa* 'Plumosa Aurea', but the pale yellowy gold of *Physocarpus opulifolius* 'Luteus' can be quite good mixed in a shrubbery; it doesn't attract too much attention.

Some of the most useful golden-leaved plants are those that do not turn green in shade, because they can give the impression of warm light in a dull part of the garden. The mock oranges are generally grown exclusively for their flowers but *Philadelphus coronarius* 'Aureus' has fragrant flowers and golden foliage that retains its warm colouring in shade. At Tintinhull we grow it in quite deep shade in rather dry soil with golden feverfew (*Chrysanthemum parthenium* 'Aureum'). The golden-leaved hop (*Humulus lupulus* 'Aureus') is another good foliage plant that will retain its colour in shade. I have even seen it growing in a London basement, planted in a pot where there is virtually no direct sunlight, but retaining its wonderful gold colour all the way up to the railing.

Climbers

Climbers are very much neglected as foliage plants despite the fact that there are some truly spectacular ones. At Tintinhull we have *Actinidia kolomikta* on a west-facing wall. Before the plant flowers, the heart-shaped leaves banded white, pink and green, make an arresting pattern. They later fade to brownish green but, while it lasts, the display is more exciting than that produced by many flowers. Perhaps even more curious is the Chinese gooseberry or kiwi fruit (*A. chinensis*). It needs a warm climate to produce fruit successfully but its vigorous hairy stems and large hairy leaves make it an attractive ornamental, and it also has a beautiful flower.

Autumn Beauty

Many of the deciduous climbers colour very well in autumn. *Vitis coignetiae*, another vigorous plant with very large leaves which, like *Actinidia chinensis*, is suitable for a pergola, turns bright red. After visiting the Loire region of France in autumn I have taken to using climbers such as Virginia creeper (*Parthenocissus quinquefolia*) and Boston ivy (*P. tricuspidata*).

Strong autumn colour, which is best on soils tending towards acidity and in regions where a hot summer is followed by sharp early frosts, does not jump out of the landscape in the way that bright foliage can do at other times of the year. There may be great differences of colour intensity but the whole landscape takes on a tonality with which the vivid reds and yellows of maples (*Acer*) and sweet gum (*Liquidambar styraciflua*) blend quite easily.

I would certainly want to have some plants principally for their autumn foliage, among them the beautiful *Cercidiphyllum japonicum*. This is an excellent tree for a small garden as its foliage is attractive at all stages from spring to autumn, and, for the large garden, the spreading *Parrotia persica*, with dying leaves of wonderfully subtle richness.

The epimediums are among the loveliest ground-covering perennials. The leaves of *E. × rubrum* are bronzy pink when they first emerge in early spring. This is a deciduous species with good autumn colour.

Herbaceous Plants

When it comes to herbaceous plants many gardeners don't think of foliage other than in terms of getting the ground covered with something that is as vigorous as weeds but is marginally more acceptable. This understanding of the use of ground cover does not take account of the great qualities of many of the plants made familiar through the writings of Graham Stuart Thomas.

One such plant I wouldn't want to be without is lady's mantle (*Alchemilla mollis*). The light green leaves, opening like miniature umbrellas, are covered with soft hairs that catch droplets of dew or rain. Like tellimas and tiarellas it is a first-rate plant for covering odd corners and when it is repeated throughout a garden it very effectively holds the planting together.

Like lady's mantle, most of the epimediums are deciduous, the new leaves – for instance, of *E. × rubrum* – beautifully tinted as they emerge. It is perfect as a rock garden plant but an evergreen species, *E. perralderanum*, which is especially useful as ground cover has leaves that take on attractive tints in the winter months. In spring, to get the full benefit of the delicate yellow flowers which are obscured by the foliage, cut off the brown leaves.

Although some of the euphorbias might do as ground cover, that is not how I think of them. They are, nonetheless, very important to my kind of gardening. At Tintinhull we have a very good form of *E. wulfenii* that is an important winter and spring foliage plant. The erect stems and narrow blue-green leaves are attractive over a long season, well before the dense heads of yellow-green bracts begin their prolonged display. The form we have comes almost true from seed and we encourage it to seed itself in the garden.

Another good euphorbia is *E. sikkimensis*, which Graham Stuart Thomas describes as having stems 'like bright red glass in early spring'. The foliage eventually turns soft green but the early growth is wonderfully tinted. There are other euphorbias with young foliage that is purplish-red (e.g., *E. amygdaloides* 'Purpurea') or bronzy (e.g., *E. palustris*), in all cases the leaves and stems making handsome combinations with the showy flower bracts. When I grow them, I prefer growing them to avoid containing them in neat clumps, but rather to let them seed about so that the lovely colour of their young foliage forms a background in the border during spring as do their very good autumn tints. There are not many border plants that colour so well at the end of the season.

The hellebores are also indispensable in winter and early spring. All have interesting foliage and many of those with green flowers are exceptionally good. The native stinking hellebore (*H. foetidus*) is a quite undemanding but handsome plant with dark deeply divided leaves that can solve the problem posed by an awkward corner. Many of the hybrids derived from *H. lividus*, itself rather tender, often show the slightly pink tinge to the leaf of the parent. A good example is *H. × sternii*, which has the hardiness of its other parent, *H. corsicus*.

I am inclined to add peonies to this miscellaneous group because many of the species have excellent foliage, though the foliage can get

A large number of herbs are attractive foliage plants and they can make very happy associations when they are brought together. However, there is plenty of scope to use herbs among other ornamentals in the garden.

rather heavy towards the end of summer and in the case of the tree peonies the dying leaves are very untidy. One of the most unusual is *P. tenuifolia*, with grassy, fennel-like leaves. The finely divided leaves of the shrubby *P. potaninii* are very elegant but perhaps one of the loveliest peonies to observe developing is *P. mlokosewitschii*, the leaves changing from red to soft green before the lemon yellow flowers open.

I am now rather bored with *P. lutea ludlowii*, but I remember early in my gardening days being given a seedling by Lady Heathcoat-Amory at Knightshayes Court and being thrilled to have a plant that I thought very good. In gardening, you sometimes think that you have grown beyond things when what has really happened is that you have become more observant about qualities and shortcomings.

Most gardeners probably have only one main border, so it makes sense to aim for a sustained display throughout the year rather than to contrive one or two spectacular but short seasons. Plants that perform more than once are invaluable. One of the most reliable is catmint, of which the best known form is probably *Nepeta* 'Six Hills Giant'. The grey-green hummocky foliage is wonderful early in the year as an edging or as a solid clump in a border. In early summer the foliage is obscured by lavender-blue flowers for many weeks. When flowering is over, the stems can be cut back and there will be a second growth of deliciously soft foliage, followed by yet another crop of flowers.

Another plant that will shoot again if cut down after flowering is the cottage-garden goat's rue (*Galega officinalis*), which makes useful clumps at the back of a border. If it is cut down by the end of June, although it won't flower a second time, you will have a wonderful mound of fresh green foliage that will carry through until the autumn. Several other old-fashioned flowers can be cut down in the same way, including Jacob's ladder (*Polemonium caeruleum*), which makes attractive tufts of elegant leaflets. A somewhat neglected plant with fern-like lacy foliage is sweet cicely (*Myrrhis odorata*). It tends to be confined to herb and kitchen gardens but is well worth growing in main borders. It is essential to cut it down after flowering to control its prolific seeding but you will then get a second flush of billowing foliage.

Ornamental Herbs

The herb garden is naturally a part of the garden where foliage is very important and some herbs are excellent used ornamentally elsewhere in the garden. The giant medicinal fennel (*Ferula tingitana*) is not unlike the common fennel (*Foeniculum vulgare*) with its very finely divided leaves but grows to 2.4 or 2.7m (8 or 9ft). It is not particularly tender but may take six years to flower, needing a hot summer in the preceding year. There is also an even more feathery species, *F. communis*.

Another herb worth growing for its foliage is the biennial angelica (*Angelica archangelica*). To keep a stock, sow every year. We have used it as a corner plant in a new border with shrub roses. The deeply dissected leaves last for almost the whole year and when the plant has finished flowering you simply throw it away.

Large-leaved Plants

There are very few foliage plants that you dispense with after a short season. One short-lived perennial that is generally grown as an annual and which produces a really handsome fan of leaves is the large tobacco plant *Nicotiana sylvestris*. It isn't scented like *N. affinis* but it is a long time before it flowers. The magnificent giant lily (*Cardiocrinum giganteum*) is in some senses similar, for the bulb dies after flowering, although it normally produces several offsets. The large, heart-shaped leaves are not a bit like those of an ordinary lily. They are arranged in a spiral till just beneath the first flower, the whole plant making a splendid spire – provided it has been well fed.

Cardiocrinum plants belong to woodland, as do the hostas, a group of large-leaved plants that have become enormously fashionable, especially in America. I do love hostas when they are planted in great masses so that you get rippling waves of foliage, always with the various kinds kept separate. However, I am not as interested in them as I was and I particularly dislike seeing them when they have not been properly looked after and are showing slug damage.

I have very mixed feelings, too, about another group of large-leaved foliage plants, bergenias, which are more suitable for drier conditions than hostas are. They can be rather coarse and sometimes look an awful mess. One that I do like, *B. stracheyi*, has little shiny leaves and attractive pink or white flowers.

Some of the best of the really large-leaved herbaceous plants – gunneras, rheums and rodgersias – need moist conditions and are not plants for the small garden. We have found that some rodgersias will do reasonably well even in our dry soil. We grow *R. aesculifolia*, *R. pinnata* and *R. podophylla*, but if I had a large pond I would want to grow *R. tabularis* and a clump of *Gunnera manicata* so that I could enjoy the phenomenal development of the vast, bristly, deeply lobed leaves each season.

In drier conditions, acanthus can make striking foliage plants. My preference is for *A. mollis latifolius*, with shiny green leaves that are nicely lobed and dissected. Last year we had here an accidental but very beautiful combination of it and *Salvia argentea*, a highly attractive biennial with the striking feature of huge furry leaves.

Grey and Silver

Many gardeners use grey and silver foliage plants in a rather cautious way, combining them, as they might white flowers, to give a safe solution to a difficult mixture of flowering colour. I am very much against using grey-leaved plants as dot plants in bedding-out schemes. I like to see grey foliage used in a mass or with particular attention paid to the plants' architectural qualities. The grey-leaved globe artichoke (*Cynara scolymus* 'Glauca') and the cardoon (*C. cardunculus*) with their imposing proportions and beautifully divided foliage of dull silver make good corner plants to frame borders. Unlike most grey-leaved plants they need rich soil. Eryngiums, on the other hand, do well in relatively poor conditions. 'Miss Willmott's ghost', *E. giganteum*, is one of the most impressive, a wonderfully jagged, silvery vertical in the border, but as it is a biennial it is a bit of a nuisance keeping the sequence going. It is a genus of which I would like to build up a collection, including species such as *E. variifolium* and the rather difficult *E. proteiflorum*. This is probably the most silvery of all but it is a plant I would not put in a border but would grow by itself in a pot and take a lot of trouble over.

For planting in groups (for instance, to get a formal effect by repetition) the artemisias are among the most useful grey-leaved plants. If only it were slightly hardier, my favourite foliage artemisia would be *A. arborescens*; the form 'Faith Raven' is hardier than the standard plant. It is incredibly useful because it grows tall in a season, making a wonderful background. Two other very good artemisias are *A. ludoviciana* 'Latifolia' and *A.* 'Powis Castle'. The latter is a very good slate grey and shapely; it rarely flowers and so tends to hold its colour.

Two less common grey foliage plants worth looking out for are *Lysimachia ephemerum* and *Convolvulus althaeoides*. We have the former in our white garden; it comes through quite early in the year and flourishes until the end of August, when it flowers and starts going back. The flowers are pinky white but it is the glaucous green foliage that goes so well with other greys and whites. The convolvulus is a twining plant from southern Europe that will romp through a border and become a pest rather easily but in a border of limited size it is worth taking the trouble for the beauty of its grey leaves, shaped very much like those of a creeping buttercup.

Variegated Foliage

When I started gardening I used a lot of plants with variegated leaves and still have an ambition to have a border entirely of variegated foliage, probably cream and green. To carry it off would be some feat. I know private gardens, where everything is either purple or variegated. Even when plants are well grown the effect can be disastrous.

There are many herbaceous and woody variegated plants that I enjoy incorporating with other plants because of the lightness they bring and because of the detailed beauty of the plants themselves. A good example of one that can be used to lighten a planted area is *Brunnera macrophylla* 'Hadspen Cream'. It is an invaluable ground cover with a very dark green leaf relieved by the creamy edge without undermining the effect of the blue flowers.

The variegated *Fatsia japonica* is a splendid plant that warrants the sort of close scrutiny it would get in a small town garden. The perfect plant for my variegated border is the mock orange *Philadelphus* 'Innocence'. It is a most beautiful example of an off-white flower (very fragrant) matching a very slight foliage variegation.

Grasses and Ferns

Two other categories of foliage plants that no gardener should neglect are the grasses and the ferns. I would very much like to grow many more grasses and bamboos than I do at present. I am inspired by a private garden near here where you push your way through rustling groves of bamboos. The graceful arching growth of grasses cannot be properly appreciated unless they are grown in clumps of reasonable size. A repetition of clumps, for instance of *Miscanthus*, is a very effective way of giving a garden a quietly formal structure and one that will carry on into the winter if the russet foliage is allowed to stand.

Many people have come to think of the pampas grasses (*Cortaderia*) as very suburban but it is the flowering tufts that are rather artifical; the foliage is very good and the plants are worth growing for this alone.

Ferns, unfortunately are something we can't grow particularly well here. We have the ordinary hart's tongue fern (*Asplenium scolopendrium*), which I love, all over the garden but virtually none of the moisture-loving species with finely divided leaves. If you have the right conditions, how lucky you are, for they are very beautiful combined with almost all other plants. If you haven't, remember that there are other plants with finely divided foliage, including astilbes, aruncus and dicentras, and these can go some way to give you the lovely patterns that you get from ferns.

Lasting Influences

As a gardener I have gone off at tangents very much according to opportunities. At Hadspen, the Edwardian garden I have mentioned, I had to put aside the influence of Italian formal gardens and concentrate on enhancing a natural woodland garden with a rather subtle blending of plant textures. It was a wonderful phase in my gardening experience and I learned an enormous amount, but I did find it very exciting coming to Tintinhull, a garden with sharp lines and clearly defined spaces. What has delighted me is that, far from abandoning the foliage plants I came to know so well at Hadspen, I am using them here but within a formal structure. They are, after all, plants that no gardener with a difference – can afford to neglect.

The Vertical Dimension

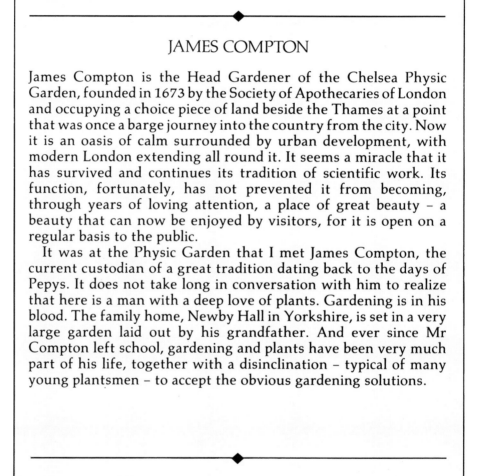

JAMES COMPTON

James Compton is the Head Gardener of the Chelsea Physic Garden, founded in 1673 by the Society of Apothecaries of London and occupying a choice piece of land beside the Thames at a point that was once a barge journey into the country from the city. Now it is an oasis of calm surrounded by urban development, with modern London extending all round it. It seems a miracle that it has survived and continues its tradition of scientific work. Its function, fortunately, has not prevented it from becoming, through years of loving attention, a place of great beauty – a beauty that can now be enjoyed by visitors, for it is open on a regular basis to the public.

It was at the Physic Garden that I met James Compton, the current custodian of a great tradition dating back to the days of Pepys. It does not take long in conversation with him to realize that here is a man with a deep love of plants. Gardening is in his blood. The family home, Newby Hall in Yorkshire, is set in a very large garden laid out by his grandfather. And ever since Mr Compton left school, gardening and plants have been very much part of his life, together with a disinclination – typical of many young plantsmen – to accept the obvious gardening solutions.

The silver-leaved pear, *Pyrus salicifolia*, has become one of the most commonly planted small weeping trees as there is room for it even in a suburban garden of modest size. It is a plant of good qualities but its popularity has been at the expense of a number of other fine small trees.

ONE OF THE UNHAPPY CONSEQUENCES of the steady reduction in the size of our gardens is that we seem to be under pressure to fill them with dwarfish plants. There is, of course, every reason to be grateful for some of the short forms of garden giants that breeders have produced and no denying the exquisite beauty of many naturally small plants, from alpine perennials and miniature bulbs to ground-hugging shrubs. But to garden exclusively with such plants, particularly where there is no change of level, even a raised bed, to give relief, makes for a curiously two-dimensional and rather dreary effect.

Trees and Shrubs

The most useful plants for giving a garden an authentic scale, and for making it look well furnished, are trees and shrubs. They are plants for the long term, their woody frame of trunk and branches sometimes build up only slowly over many years, but how much poorer our gardens would be without them. It is not simply that they lift the eye above ground level, with their upright, domed or weeping habit; they give a garden weight and substance.

In the rush for instant effect – another of the less attractive developments in modern gardening – there is a danger that the value of long-term plants will be overlooked completely. We need some of the confidence and patience of the great landscapists of the eighteenth century, who were able to visualize their spindly saplings as mature belts and clumps of trees. Gardeners, in fact, are almost always surprised by the speed with which trees and shrubs grow. The case for being wary of very fast growers is strong, for their vices can easily outweigh a single advantage.

Value and Versatility

The value of trees and shrubs, of course, goes well beyond giving a garden a proper sense of scale and a feeling of maturity. Their height and density allow them to be used singly or in groups, informally or as clipped hedging, to provide protection from cold winds, creating sheltered zones that make being outdoors agreeable and where more tender plants might flourish. It is difficult to overstate the value of trees as windbreaks in some parts of Britain, particularly near the coast. The magnificent garden at Tresco Abbey, in the Isles of Scilly, demonstrates what can be achieved in a very windy location provided there are adequate shelter belts. In the original planting the evergreen conifers used here were the Monterey cypress (*Cupressus macrocarpa*) and the Monterey pine (*Pinus radiata*), both tolerant of salt-laden air.

In a very different kind of environment – urban areas or where houses and offices are close to busy roads – trees and shrubs can help to screen out unwanted noise. Obviously, if the planting is for this purpose, evergreens should be chosen.

In a world that, sadly, tends to become more ugly rather than more beautiful, plants are also called upon to screen out the unsightly, which can be just as much a problem in a quiet rural retreat as in a built-up area. Power pylons and the brutal architecture of modern farming spoil many a view. When faced with an eyesore, the temptation is to opt for whatever is fastest growing. It is, as always, worth pausing for a moment and, instead of replacing the unsightly with something that will always be unsatisfactory, to choose something less speedy that will increasingly be a pleasure to the eye.

The very best reason for planting trees and shrubs is not a matter of function or use, but of the quality and beauty of the plants themselves. It is very difficult sometimes to discover the secret of a plant's appeal, for the sum of the individual features – leaf, flower, fruit and habit – is very much greater than the parts. This is something that occasionally strikes one very forcefully quite out of the blue, for instance, when watching a tree heaving in a storm or listening to the murmur of leaves rustled by a gentle breeze. The way in which a particular tree or shrub moves and the sound it makes are not features that are normally included in catalogue descriptions. One can hardly expect such a description to convey all the qualities of a living thing; to appreciate these, you need to see plants growing. Fortunately, in Britain there are many gardens and collections of outstanding quality where it is possible to see mature specimens of rare as well as common trees.

Factors to Consider

I will mention later a few among the many that I would like to include in my own paradise garden, but would first make the point that if you only have room for one or two trees or large shrubs it is worth looking for those with multiple virtues. You don't want something that has just got lovely flowers for a week or two each year and for the rest of the time is

A tree has to have multiple virtues to warrant its inclusion in a small garden. And the fact that it will create shade is a major factor to be borne in mind when considering where it should be planted. A fruit tree can be a good solution to the problem of scale posed by a small garden. With apples, cropping is improved by cross-pollination so that you need at least a pair. The quince, *Cydonia oblonga*, is a very attractive spreading small tree that is self-fertile.

97

rather nondescript. The ideal of a deciduous tree that is neat, handsome in foliage, beautiful in flower, colourful in fruit and autumn foliage and elegant when bare in winter may take some finding but it is the sort of plant that the gardener with limited space should be looking for.

My paradise garden will, I hope, be somewhat larger than a small suburban rectangle. Even here at the Chelsea Physic Garden, there is not room for many trees. Yet I have become acquainted with so many interesting species and varieties, particularly in the last ten or fifteen years. My fascination with unusual, not necessarily rare but less familiar, plants has been nurtured all my life. The garden at my family home, Newby Hall in Yorkshire, contains a very wide range of plants grown with great style in a splendid setting. And as a child I was taken round other gardens by knowledgeable and enthusiastic parents; even when one didn't participate graciously, a lot rubbed off. Training and work in horticulture, getting to know well collections such as those at Kew, where I was a student, have all consolidated my early experience.

But I have seen gardens that are a warning against collecting plants simply because they are unusual. Such curio gardens, crammed with the contorted, variegated and unnatural, make one long for something as simple as a drive lined with snowdrops, daffodils in an orchard or clumps of unpretentious box.

For me, one of the great pleasures of gardening is that it is such a common-sense business. You see people who have never had much experience of gardening in their lives suddenly discovering that it is not a practice veiled in mysteries. Common sense is certainly what you need when planting trees and shrubs; you must not rush to hasty decisions. You need to take into account quite matter-of-fact restrictions. For instance, there may be overhead telegraph wires and power cables or underground drains or electricity, gas and water supplies that a mature tree will interfere with. And there are, too, buildings and walls the foundations of which may be damaged by large shrubs and trees planted too close. There is a particular risk on clay soils, where the expansion and contraction of the plastic material exaggerated by a tree sucking moisture from the ground can cause serious problems. For example, in parts of London that are built on clay, problems of subsidence often occur after long hot summers like that of 1976. Unfortunately, there is plenty of evidence that some people don't have common sense for you do see weeping willows planted just a few feet from dining-room windows.

It is a fact also that trees and large shrubs create shade, although the density varies very much from one kind of plant to another, and they take up a lot of moisture and nutrients from the soil. When you are putting in large permanent plants you have to decide what it is you want from your garden. There is no point in planting trees where they might cast shade on a sunny spot that you have earmarked for making into a paved area for sitting out, or on an open, fertile piece of ground that you want to use for growing vegetables and fruit. Also a limited range of plants thrives in dry shade so – if you hope in the long term to have a flowering border in dappled shade – you have got to choose the right sort of canopy, not a dense evergreen but perhaps one of the lightly foliaged birches.

Climbers

The case for growing climbers doesn't rest simply on the fact that they are useful plants for giving height in gardens where shrubs and trees might create too much. Though their versatility makes them particularly useful in the small garden, they are plants full of interest and appeal in their own right.

With climbers, it is a matter of being opportunist with some of the great opportunists of the plant world. Most of them, woody and herbaceous, are speedy growers that rush to the light, supporting themselves on whatever is available, generally free-standing trees and shrubs. They are equipped in various ways to take advantage of whatever support is available. Some, such as the wisterias, have twining stems that in the wild work their way round the trunks and branches of trees, sometimes carrying the plant 9–12m (30–40ft). Others, particularly among the herbaceous climbers such as members of the pea family, have tendrils that make elegant twists around supports, allowing the plant to hoist itself up. Some of the untidier

Many fine climbers clothe the old walls at Sissinghurst in Kent. *Clematis montana* is a very vigorous and free-flowering species. The flowering of this clematis to provide a background to a magnolia at its peak is a typical refinement of this garden.

scrambling plants, such as roses, use hooks to tangle themselves in the growth of another plant or to cling to rough surfaces. Ivies and several other highly ornamental climbers have aerial roots by which they fasten on to any available surface.

To grow climbers successfully you must give them adequate support. It is quite possible in a garden setting to encourage some to scramble among other plants much as they do in the wild. An old fruit tree supporting a climbing rose, for instance the slightly tender *Rosa longicuspis*, has become a gardening cliché but is, nonetheless, a very successful way of bringing new life to a mature feature of a garden. The flame creeper (*Tropaeolum speciosum*) never looks more beautiful than when its brilliant flowers are offset by a dark background of yew. And many of the less hearty clematis (I am excluding the lovely but rampant *C. montana*) are seen to perfection draped over a vigorous shrub.

Against walls, self-clinging climbers such as ivies and *Hydrangea petiolaris* will not need additional support, although it often helps with these plants to give them a little steadying support until they begin to cling. There is, by the way, very little evidence of either of these plants causing damage to a sound wall, although the aerial roots of Virginia creeper (*Parthenocissus quinquefolia*) and its near relatives do get into the

The spectacular effect of this laburnum tunnel is not for the small garden – it occupies too much space and the season of magic is too brief. It is, however, the kind of theatrical *tour de force* worth planning for the larger garden, using architectural features clothed with climbers or trained plants.

pointing and eventually can cause a lot of damage. They are still beautiful plants; the autumn red of Virginia creeper against yellowy white limestone as you see it in the Cotswolds is a really lovely sight.

For those climbers that are not self-clinging you have to provide trellis, netting or wires as support and your choice should be dictated as much by aesthetic and practical factors as by considerations of cost. If you have got to get at a wall, for example to paint it, you might consider detachable or hinged trellis. At the Chelsea Physic Garden we have some lovely old high walls that have supported plants for a very long time. Here we use galvanized wire supported by vine eyes. With some wall shrubs and climbers, including roses, you will need to tie them in to their supports; this is something to bear in mind if you have a thickly planted border in front of a wall.

Another possibility with climbers is to use them to clothe architectural features in the garden, such as arches and pergolas. The popularity of the pergola has waned since the Edwardian period, perhaps because of the expense of maintenance, perhaps because there sometimes doesn't seem much point in creating any more shade than is absolutely necessary in a British garden. We don't have the same need for it as they do, say, in Mediterranean countries. However, the renewed interest in formal gardening may mean that these architectural features will be used more widely once more. Both arches and pergolas certainly introduce height and an element of theatricality to a garden but they need a clothing of climbers to give them a mature look. Remember that if you use deciduous climbers there will be clearing up to do in autumn.

Making a Selection

So far I have spoken in a very general way about finding a place in the garden for two broad categories of plants. In many ways I am reluctant to be more specific, to give any selection of plants that is not related to the requirements of a specific garden, taking into account its peculiarities of soil and micro-climate. What suits the light sandy soil and remarkably mild micro-climate of the Physic Garden, for example, many not thrive in many other gardens even within the London area. The ground here slopes down to the Thames so that the frost can drain away and yet we are almost at sea level.

It is a real luxury being able to plan the planting of a garden; it is something to be savoured, not something to be rushed into. All other considerations set to one side, there are quite simply thousands of plants from which to choose. It has not always been so. Even Philip Miller, who was appointed Gardener (he would now be called Curator) of the Physic Garden in 1722 and became one of the greatest botanical horticulturalists of his period, would be astonished at what he could now add to his celebrated *Dictionary of Gardening*. Botanists and speculative plant-hunters have scoured the temperate world – often at great personal risk – to give us the choice we now enjoy. True, the stock of many garden centres does not reflect the astounding richness of that choice but there are specialist nurseries that cater for the discriminating gardener and it is worth seeking them out.

Interesting Leaf Shapes

My selection for a paradise garden would begin with deciduous trees chosen for their interesting leaf shape. For instance, I would like to have the maidenhair tree (*Ginkgo biloba*), with its curious fan-shaped leaves that turn lemon-yellow in autumn. The fact that in some senses it is a living fossil, the only surviving representatives of a primitive order that botanists have placed between the conifers and cycads adds to its particular appeal.

I would also like some of the cut-leaved forms of common trees, such as the cut-leaved beech (*Fagus sylvatica heterophylla*), which is to me very familiar from my childhood but which one rarely sees in cultivation. Among other trees that I would want for their attractive leaf shape (and for many other virtues, including modest size) is *Malus trilobata*, which at a quick glance might be taken for a maple rather than an apple. The Judas tree (*Cercis siliquastrum*) also ought to find a place for, despite its sombre legend (it is one of the trees on which Judas is said to have hanged himself) and its untidy habit, I would want it for its unusual leaf shape, rounded but heart-shaped at the base. In the year following a hot summer it will sometimes produce a profuse display of flowers.

Flowering Trees and Shrubs

When it comes to choosing trees and shrubs for the quality of their flowers, the range is so enormous that it is impossible to make a selection that is in any sense useful. The flowering evergreens are in themselves an enormous category, including such popular groups as the camellias and rhododendrons. Among deciduous flowering trees there are two genera that deserve special consideration, the magnolias and the cherries. Among the magnolias there is scarcely one that is not worth consideration. The giant *M. campbelli* and some of the other tall-growing species and hybrids would give a garden real distinction, although you may need to be patient for some of them to reach flowering age. Fortunately for owners of smaller gardens there are more compact magnolias, such as *M. kobus*, *M. stellata* and 'Leonard Messel', a magnificient pink-flowered hybrid, apparently the result of a chance cross at Nymans in Sussex. Another good magnolia for the smaller garden and one with fragrant flowers is *M. salicifolia*.

The cherries include some quite ugly plants. I have an aversion for the widely planted 'Kanzan', with flowers that are the strident pink of tart's pants and hence the name by which it is known in my family. But there are other delicate and very beautiful plants such as *P. triloba* and the cheering autumn cherry (*P. subhirtella* 'Autumnalis'). A plant of this quality that flowers in the dead of winter must have a special value. It is sometimes said that the flowering season of the cherries is very short but so many of them have other qualities in addition to the beauty of their flowers; *P. mume* and *P.* 'Okame', two small cherries, have interesting foliage and good autumn colouring, while *P. serrula* has very attractive bark.

Autumn Colour

There are many deciduous trees that are worth cultivating for the wonderful autumn colouring of their foliage. There are obvious choices such as *Liquidambar styraciflua* and *Nyssa sylvatica* or the smaller and more lime-tolerant *N. sinensis*. *Parrotia persica* is a spreading dome-shaped tree with leaves that go through a lovely progression of colour changes in autumn but, if you have the space, it is also worth growing for its strange tufty crimson flowers that appear before the leaves, and a flaking bark, not unlike that of a London plane. It thus provides you with a number of effects, all of which are attractive in their own right.

The maples are, of course, outstanding for their autumn colour although they need sheltered positions if the delicate foliage is not to be damaged by cold winds in spring and most need acid soils. *Acer rubrum* is reasonably lime tolerant but colours best on acid soils. It owes its specific name, I think, to its interesting flowers rather than to the red-tinted autumn foliage. To return to my theme of finding more than one positive quality in a plant: in *Malus coronaria* you have a crab with many virtues. It makes a sturdy, well-shaped small tree with large fragrant flowers of delicate pink in spring and richly coloured foliage in the autumn, both of which are extremely striking.

The autumn colouring of foliage is especially intense on soils tending to acid and when a hot summer is followed by early frosts. Many deciduous trees and shrubs are worth growing for their autumn foliage but for the small garden you need to select plants that perform well at other times of the year, too.

Ornamental Fruits

Good autumn foliage is also often accompanied by highly ornamental fruit. One tree that should certainly feature in the paradise garden is the quince (*Cydonia oblonga*), with highly aromatic, pear-shaped fruits that are not only ornamental but also of great culinary value. It is a very attractive and sadly underplanted tree, with attractive pink flowers in spring and good autumn colouring. Even if it is only represented by the native rowan (*Sorbus acuparia*) the *Sorbus* genus should certainly be included, but among other species and hybrids to look for are *S. hupehensis*, with white fruits, *S.* 'Joseph Rock', an outstanding cultivar with reddish-yellow fruits, and *S. poteriifolia*, with pink fruit. The crabs (*Malus*) as well as the members of the *Sorbus* genus are perhaps obvious plants to include on account of their fruits. To represent the many less familiar fruiting plants I will mention *Decaisnea fargesii*, which will eventually build up a clump of many stems, in autumn supporting immense, dangling blue-grey fruits with black seeds bursting through.

Valuable Evergreens

Of evergreens, I would not want too strong a representation of conifers, although for a large woodland or wild setting there are certainly beautiful species such as *Picea brewerana* and *P. smithiana* that deserve inclusion. In a garden setting, those that I like best are of erect habit, such as *Juniperus virginiana* 'Skyrocket' and *Cupressus sempervirens* 'Stricta'. The evergreens I particularly like include some very homely plants such as the shrubby box (*Buxus sempervirens*), whether it is grown naturally or clipped and shaped, and holly (species and cultivars of *Ilex*), which is such a splendid shelter plant. But I would also want some evergreens with unusual qualities of foliage, such as silvery-leaved species of *Elaeagnus*, for example *E. macrophylla* and the semi-evergreen *E. angustifolia* or variegated cultivars of plants such as *Osmanthus heterophyllus*.

Variety of Habit

All other qualities set on one side, I would want a collection to contain trees and shrubs of different habit. Some would have to be dome-shaped, like the strawberry tree (*Arbutus unedo*), others spreading like the witch hazel (*Hamamelis mollis*); some should be fastigiate, like the small columnar cherry *Prunus* 'Amanogawa', or weeping, like the silver-leaved pear (*Pyrus salicifolia*). A jumbled collection would, of course, be a disaster but the paradise garden, I am assuming, allows me scope to arrange the most pleasing effects.

Some Climbers of Distinction

When it comes to choosing climbers, the major distinction to make is between those, many of them slightly tender, that benefit from the protection and warmth of a south- or west-facing wall and those that are sufficiently tough for east- and north-facing positions. Wisterias and roses are typical of many plants that will do reasonably well on cold walls although they will flower very much better when they get sun directly on them. The climbing hydrangea (*Hydrangea petiolaris*) is often recommended for north-facing walls and excellent it is but other very good plants are equally worth growing and some are self-clinging. Three that deserve to be much more widely grown are *Decumaria sinensis*, *Pileostegia viburnoides* and *Schizophragma integrifolia*, all of them flowering plants with interesting foliage.

For warm walls there is a splendid choice to try outside the conventional range. A good starting point would be the abutilons, *A. megapotamicum*, a small shrub with yellow and red flowers, and the rather larger *A. vitifolium* with wide saucer-shaped flowers. One of my favourites is *Solanum jasminiodes* 'Album', a member of the potato family that gives a wonderful display from mid-summer until the onset of cold weather in autumn.

Tall Herbaceous Plants

We started by talking about the way different plants can be used to introduce vertical interest in the garden and we have looked very briefly at trees, shrubs and climbers. To finish I would like to make the point that there are a number of very tall herbaceous plants that are well worth growing to give height in borders. The obvious plants are dahlias and delphiniums but there are lots of others to consider. There are the lush plants that thrive in moist soil, such as gunneras, ligularias and rheums, and rather more surprisingly those that do well in ordinary even quite dry conditions. Two to consider that are not widely grown are the giant fennel (*Ferula communis* 'Gigantea'), which can reach a height of 3.6m (12ft), and the prairie dock (*Silphium terebinthinaceum*), which has large, really handsome foliage, although the flowers don't count for much. Borders, like every other part of the garden, need variations of height and some good tall plants if they are not to seem dull and ordinary. Fortunately there are many plants that will add stature and distinction to the overall effect.

Trees, shrubs and climbers are not the only plants that lift the garden out of two dimensions. In a well-planned border there is a gradation of heights, with a backing of really tall plants. In this border at Nymans in West Sussex, dahlias top a well-grown collection of bedding plants.

105

Roses Old and New

MICHAEL GIBSON

No truly English garden would be complete without its roses – and Michael Gibson is without question the doyen of contemporary rose authorities. Not only is the rose a very important category of ornamentals and one that contains a wide variety of plant and flower types; it is simply popular. It is almost the very first plant the novice gardener wants and few connoisseurs of garden plants would be happy without one or two at least.

Michael Gibson is exceptionally well placed to comment on the best ways to grow roses and on the performance of individual varieties. He has grown a very large number himself, is an authority on the history of the rose and has written extensively about old and new varieties. For many years he has been a member of the Council of the Royal National Rose Society (he has received the Society's highest award, the Dean Hole Medal) and has recently been its President. His love of his subject comes across clearly in every word he speaks or writes on it; his devotion to roses is demonstrated in one of his current projects, a mammoth survey of the rose gardens of England, which involves him criss-crossing the country to visit both private and public gardens. One of the things this will provide, he says, is a fascinating insight into the way roses perform in different growing conditions.

Many of the great gardens in Britain contain important collections of roses, including old varieties and species as well as modern kinds. The collection at Castle Howard in North Yorkshire is justly famous. Here roses are underplanted with deliciously scented pinks.

IN BRITAIN, THE ROSE ENJOYS A SPECIAL PRESTIGE as an ornamental, but its development as a garden flower is far from being a uniquely British achievement. British nurserymen and gardeners have played an important part, particularly since the middle of the last century, in breeding and growing the tens of thousands of known varieties, but the story of the rose goes back further than the story of mankind. It was the rose in history that first caught my imagination. I was fascinated to discover how frequently the rose has featured in art, commerce, literature, mythology and religion over the years; it comes into almost every aspect of man's activities.

I have gone on to discover how roses perform as garden plants, through growing them myself and by observing them growing in a wide range of conditions, in other countries as well as in Britain. That experience has constantly confirmed my admiration for a plant of outstanding qualities. The species and cultivars are wonderfully varied in size, habit, foliage and fruit, flower colour, form and scent. What has disappointed me more often than the performance of individual plants is the way gardeners sometimes fail to make the best use of roses, limiting themselves unnecessarily to one category or to a single manner of growing them. There have been several shifts in fashion in the way that roses are grown, and perhaps the present tendency to combine them with other flowers and foliage plants will give way once again to a more formal treatment in isolation. However, the average garden is too small for that, even if there were not obvious advantages in planting roses with other good ornamentals.

Classification

The ordinary gardener is in the fortunate position of being able to stand back and let the experts worry about the problems of classification. After all, roses have not developed to conform to a clearly defined system. The categories that have been devised are but an attempt to create order from an incredibly muddled history of hybridization. Some of it has occurred in the wild and much of it in cultivation – accidentally as well as in controlled conditions.

Whatever the system of classification, it is inevitable that, with such a complex ancestry, there are roses that do not fit neatly into any one category. The modern bedding roses used to be (and in many catalogues still are) divided into two categories: The hybrid teas were those with long flower stems carrying a single large bloom or perhaps a main bloom with several side buds, each flower consisting of numerous petals forming a characteristically high-centred, conical shape. The floribundas bore their smaller flowers in trusses, their appeal lying in their long, colourful display, rather than in the form and the quality of their individual flowers.

In the post-war period, however, it became increasingly difficult to assign bedding roses to one or other of these two categories. The breeding of new cultivars with intermediate characteristics blurred the boundaries between them. 'Fragrant Cloud' and 'Queen Elizabeth' are but two examples.

A new classification of roses adopted by the World Federation of Rose Societies in the early 1970s, attempted to distinguish more precisely the groups of roses that are in cultivation. Modern bedding roses again fall into two main categories: Large-flowered bush roses and Cluster-flowered bush roses. There are separate categories, too, for: Modern shrub roses, Miniature Climbers, and Old garden roses that pre-dated the hybrid teas, and finally, species or roses very close to species, which in this classification are referred to as wild roses.

This is a brave attempt but it has not solved the problems that the very mixed ancestry of roses creates for the tidy mind. There is still no satisfactory way of describing in-between roses, such as the bedding roses that fall between the large-flowered and the cluster-flowered, or the miniatures that fall between the true original miniatures and the floribundas with which they have been crossed to obtain a broader range of colour.

Partly because of these shortcomings, partly because people are reluctant to accept change, the new classification has met some resistance, so that you now find both systems used, often in tandem. The ordinary gardener can take heart from the fact that the appeal of a rose is not reduced by such considerations.

Selecting Roses

When selecting the roses you want, their classification and descriptions in catalogues are only starting points. Illustrations can be helpful or quite misleading; and often they give only a superficial impression of the whole plant as opposed to the flower.

The best way to assess the suitability of a rose for your purpose is to

There is no single solution to the successful use of roses in the garden. A billowing mass of soft colour will appeal to many gardeners, but others will prefer to use roses more formally, perhaps exploiting a more vibrant range of colour.

see a mature specimen (at least three years old) growing outdoors, preferably where you know something about the growing conditions. The roses that you see at Chelsea and other major shows are not always a helpful guide because they have been pot-grown in a greenhouse, protected from the perils to which garden roses are exposed and, quite commonly, untypical in foliage and flower colour (roses grown under glass tend to be more intense in colour than they are when grown out in the open).

As I discovered while visiting important rose gardens in Britain recently, growing conditions make a great difference to the way roses behave. An example that is often quoted is, to me, one of the loveliest of the cluster-flowered or floribunda roses: the soft salmon-orange 'Elizabeth of Glamis'. I garden in Surrey on quick-draining sandy soil that is very typical of the county and here this rose performs well, making sturdy plants with good foliage that is no more disease prone than that of any other variety. Yet on heavy cold soils it can be very susceptible to disease and with die-back a common problem, so that some nurseries refuse to stock it because they cannot be confident that gardeners will have success with it.

An example from another category is the shrub rose 'Agnes'. This is an oddity in being a yellow-flowered rugosa. Almost all the hybrids derived from the oriental species *R. rugosa* have white, pink or carmine flowers. In the past I have described 'Agnes' as a straggly plant with rather poor flowers but, recently, I have seen it in several gardens – including Queen Mary's Rose Garden in Regent's Park, London – making a magnificent display.

To my mind any nursery that aims to be fair to its customers must have a show garden. Most now do and every effort is made to offer customers an adequate information service. In the last ten years there have been dramatic changes in the rose trade. The sale of bare-root stock by mail order has dwindled while the over-the-counter sale of container-grown plants has increased sharply.

Don't be misled into thinking that a young plant in a container gives any idea of the ultimate size a rose will be; check that what you are getting really is a container-grown plant, not something that has had its roots trimmed at the end of the selling season and been dumped into a container. If well-rooted, the plant should not yield if given a gentle tug.

Hybrid Teas and Floribundas

Despite an increasing interest in other groups of roses, the hybrid teas and the floribundas still remain the most popular. (I deliberately use the old terminology here, to set these categories in their historical context.) To many gardeners, the high-centred shape of the hybrid teas is the classic form of the rose but this is really a relatively recent development. 'La France', which was introduced in 1867, was the first officially recognized hybrid tea, although there were other roses of about the same period that might be considered the first of their kind. 'La France' and its competitors were the result of crossing the reasonably re-montant hybrid perpetuals, a group combining China rose blood with

that of the slightly recurrent autumn damask (*R. × damascena semper-florens*), and the then newly arrived tea roses. The tea roses brought a fresh introduction of China rose blood, improving the flowering performance and, although themselves rather tender, helped to produce a hardy race while passing on some of the refinement and delicate beauty of their flowers.

The floribundas also derive from China hybrids but these were crossed with the dense-growing *R. multiflora (R. polyantha)* to produce, in the first instance, polyantha pompon roses with their clusters of comparatively small flowers. Further crossing with hybrid teas and tea roses created a healthy strain with larger flowers in a wide range of colours, which were initially known as hybrid polyanthas. It was not until the 1940s that the American term 'floribunda', was adopted by rose breeders in Britain.

The hybrid teas and the floribundas are best used separated from other flowers. A major factor in this is that, although they have blooms of outstanding beauty, they are not beautiful plants – their growth is rather awkwardly stiff and upright. It is difficult to mask the ungainliness of the individual plant but, when planted in groups, interest is held, in the case of the hybrid teas, by a succession of refined individual blooms and, in the case of the floribundas, by the solid mass of colour formed by a multitude of small flowers.

There is often rather heated debate about whether you should mix varieties and, for that matter, whether hybrid teas and floribundas should be combined. My own practice is probably not typical and should not serve as a model to other gardeners. As I write a lot about roses and prefer to draw on direct experience, I try to grow as many roses as I can and therefore mix them up rather a lot in my garden. Even so, I would aim to plant in groups of say, four or five of any one kind, avoiding juxtaposing groups with clashing colours, such as the strong cerise pink 'Wendy Cussons' right next to the bright crimson 'Alec's Red'.

Although hybrid teas and floribundas are not easy to mix with other plants, it is not uncommon to see gardens where modern bush roses are combined happily with perennials and shrubs.

However, there is no reason why you cannot accommodate both these colours in your garden – simply separate them by a pale rose, or perhaps even by a white one such as 'Pascali'.

One argument for not mixing varieties is that some may come into flower much earlier than others creating a rather spotty effect. A more serious point, if you are trying to grow roses in a formal way, is that varieties grow to very different heights and this can create a very odd impression in a bed. However, the fact that bedding roses do grow to different heights can also be an advantage, when thoughtfully managed, providing the variation that can save a bedding scheme from appearing montonous. Taller varieties can be grouped at the back of a bed or in the centre of a square or circular one. You can even make more of the height variation by combining standards with bush roses, either repeating the same variety or introducing another with a complementary contrasting colour.

Bedding may be the most effective way of using most of the hybrid teas and floribundas but the particular qualities of some of the roses in these two categories make them highly suitable for other uses as well. For example, 'Iceberg', an enormously popular floribunda, does best when only lightly pruned. If it is allowed to develop into a plant of 1.2m (4ft) or so it makes a lovely specimen shrub, producing tiers of white flowers in great profusion. It can also be used as a hedging plant, as can another unusual and sometimes awkward floribunda, 'Queen Elizabeth'. This is not really suitable as a bedding rose at all but it will make a tall hedge, up to about 2.4m (8ft) and it also makes a handsome show at the back of a border.

Choosing hybrid teas
I am often asked what varieties of hybrid teas and floribundas I would recommend and there is a point to make here about the varieties

Floribundas, in the modern classification cluster-flowered bush roses, bloom freely over a long season and are ideal roses for bedding. Rope swags provide an elegant support for ramblers with pliant stems.

commonly seen at shows. Although hybrid teas such as 'Admiral Rodney', 'Bonsoir' and 'Champion' are frequently successful on the show bench they are not good roses in the garden. 'Admiral Rodney' and 'Champion' are not free-flowing enough and 'Bonsoir', like many very full varieties which are suitable for exhibition, does not stand up to wet weather conditions at all well. To pick out just a few for comment seems unfair to many excellent varieties, but in selecting four of each I hope to demonstrate some of the most important qualities that can be found in these two categories.

Among the hybrid teas one that must be included is 'Grandpa Dickson', which was introduced in 1966. Unlike the examples I have already mentioned, this hybrid tea is equally good as an ordinary garden variety and for exhibition. Provided that it has good growing conditions, it will produce large, soft yellow, double blooms of classic shape with extraordinary freedom. These will stand up to rough weather very well and the glossy foliage is disease free. 'Just Joey', introduced in 1973, is not a rose for the show bench but the large coppery pink ruffled petals, which are unaffected by wet weather, make this a very good choice for the flower arranger. There is some scent and the bushes make healthy vigorous growth, larger than 'Grandpa Dickson' but only average in height for this group of roses.

An even more remarkable rose from the 1970s is 'Silver Jubilee', introduced in 1978 and proving itself one of the best bedding roses. It, too, has flowers of exhibition standard, peachy pink and borne in great profusion. It may take some time to settle down but it is an exceptionally healthy variety for the ordinary garden and the well-formed flowers, unfortunately light on scent, are good as cut flowers. 'Alec's Red', the last of the four, dates from 1970. This is a bedding rose producing a wonderful succession of weather-resistant vigorous crimson flowers. This is certainly a variety of exceptional merit, counting among its virtues a healthy constitution and a strong sweet scent.

Floribundas

I have already mentioned three fine floribunda roses but as this is the most popular category and one where breeders have concentrated their attention, here is a selection of four more to match the hybrid teas.

'Anne Harkness', a relatively new introduction, dating from 1980, has been enthusiastically received by exhibitors as well as ordinary gardeners. The buff yellow, double flowers are of medium size but borne in large trusses on a tall healthy bush. It is late coming into flower but this can be used to advantage in order to fill a gap that occurs while other roses pause.

'City of Leeds', introduced in 1966, has proved to be a remarkably free-flowering variety with large, salmon-pink blooms. These may show some spotting after rain but this fault cannot detract from the plant's overall quality.

A shortcoming of many of the floribundas is that they have very little scent but 'Korresia', introduced in 1974, is a fragrant variety with yellow flowers that hold their colour well. This outstandingly healthy rose may eventually take the place of another good yellow-flowered variety, 'Allgold'.

'Memento', on the other hand, has a colour very much its own. This introduction of 1978 has salmon-red blooms that are prolific throughout the summer months. Its sustained flowering, resistance to disease and good colour make this a very good bedding rose.

As a final point on the hybrid teas and floribundas it has to be said that a number of varieties that have enjoyed great popularity now seem to be suffering from loss of vigour and are no longer as resistant to disease. In the 1960s, 'Super Star' was an exceptionally healthy rose but it is now very prone to disease; even if one liked its intense radiant colour, it would not be a rose to seek out and plant. 'Fragrant Cloud' is among other great roses that have suffered a similar decline. This sad and mysterious deterioration of some varieties, perhaps more marked among the highly bred bedding roses than in other categories, makes it important to get up-to-date information on the standing of a variety before selecting it for the garden. It is sometimes tempting for sentimental reasons to persist with varieties that are well past their best. On the whole it is better to take a hard line rather than to have the garden filled with disease-ravaged plants that bear little relation to the roses in one's memory.

Modern Shrub Roses

In the new classification, shrub roses developed since the turn of the century form one large category. Inevitably, the roses belonging to it are far from homogeneous. That is what makes this a particularly interesting group, full of varieties with great potential. Many of these roses combine happily with other shrubs and perennials in mixed borders. Quite a few are suitable for specimen planting, either singly or in groups. There are tall and short varieties that make attractive hedges, and some that can be trained as climbers.

The roses in this group tend to be rather neglected by gardeners, it being firmly, but wrongly, fixed in people's minds that they are, without exception, too big and flower only once. The character of these roses is so diverse that all one can do here is to give a hint of the riches that the adventurous gardener can find.

Rugosa Roses

The rugosas are one tribe within this group showing a marked family resemblance, typical hybrids having tough, healthy foliage and sweetly scented flowers borne over a long period. 'Roseraie de l'Hay', the finest of all the rugosas, is densely clothed in bright green leaves right to the ground and carries clusters of semi-double or double wine-red flowers, sometimes from late spring until the beginning of winter. These flowers will not last when cut (this is true for most rugosa flowers) but they are deliciously fragrant on the bush. This variety can make a tall dense and, on account of its villainous spines, forbidding hedge but it needs plenty of room for it will grow to a height of 2.4m(8ft)and makes a hedge at least 1.2m (4ft) thick.

Another outstanding rugosa, 'Scabrosa' is slightly less vigorous than 'Roseraie de l'Hay' and has very large single flowers of a soft fuchsia pink. As with most of the single rugosas, its flowers are followed by highly decorative hips, which are large, round and bright red. These are a feature, too, of the best rugosa for the small garden, 'Frau Dagmar Hartopp' (also listed as 'Fru Dagmar Hastrup'), which normally grows to 1.2m (4ft) or 1.5m (5ft) and carries a long succession of delicately veined, pale pink flowers.

These are perhaps the pick of the rugosas but another that is still popular is 'Blanc Double de Coubert', which grows to 1.8m (6ft) and has pure white papery flowers. These can be spoiled by wet weather but they are borne so freely that this is a minor problem. Hips may begin to form but do not develop. Of this group, it is the least satisfactory for informal hedging but can be very effective in a mixed border where the bareness of its base can be masked by planting.

Hybrids

The rugosa roses are closer to their species parent than many of the roses commonly grown in gardens. Among others that are close to the wild roses are several hybrids raised by the German breeder Wilhelm Kordes. One of his most remarkable successes is 'Frühlingsmorgen', a cross between the Scotch rose and a large-flowered variety, which has produced a bushy shrub with small grey-green leaves. It grows to a height of about 1.8m (6ft) and in early summer carries single scented flowers of exceptional beauty. The soft pink melting to a centre of pale yellow and a cluster of maroon stamens is of a refined simplicity that puts this rose in the very first rank. There is a second crop of flowers but not it is on the scale of the abundant early summer showing.

'Frühlingsmorgen' is the only one of the Frühlings group raised by Kordes that is remontant, but among the others there are some beautiful flowers, of which 'Frühlingsgold' is probably the best. It

'Frühlingsmorgen', an outstandingly beautiful modern shrub rose, is one of the very hardy hybrids bred by Wilhelm Kordes. The main flowering season is in early summer and there is a smaller one in autumn.

makes an enormously vigorous arching shrub, and if you have the space it is worth growing for its gloriously scented semi-double creamy-yellow flowers.

'Frühlingsgold' is not for the small garden, but 'Golden Wings', which has a Scotch rose ancestor two generations back, is of a manageable size, growing to about 1.5 × 1.5m (5 × 5ft) and has the great advantage of carrying its large single yellow flowers right through summer into autumn. To help maintain the succession of sweetly fragrant flowers, remove the hips as they form; they are not ornamental as are those of the rugosas.

'Nevada' and its sport, 'Marguerite Hilling', are large arching shrubs, reaching a height of 1.8m (6ft) and spreading as much as 2.4m (8ft) but they are outstanding varieties, in full flower making spectacular specimen plants. The semi-double flowers of 'Nevada' are creamy-white and those of 'Marguerite Hilling' are pink tinged pale yellow at the centre. The main summer display is exceptionally profuse; the second flush less generous and rather unpredictable.

For those with small gardens 'Angelina' is a very attractive alternative. It makes a healthy rounded bush not more than 1.2m (4ft) high and over a long season carries a good crop of cupped, semi-double, carmine pink flowers with a white centre and golden stamens.

Better known than this relatively recent introduction are the hybrid musks, a group developed early this century by the Rev. Joseph Pemberton. Their name is rather misleading for these roses are only tenuously connected to the true musk rose but, they are still a very beautiful group, tending to be rather lax in growth but suitable for hedging, particularly if given support by being grown between two rows of wires. Their reputation for continuity of flowering is not fully justified but dead-heading will help to encourage a new crop.

'Prosperity' is one of the most reliably recurrent and carries large trusses of fragrant, creamy white flowers that are densely petalled. 'Cornelia' is another good variety with small, very double flowers that are pink with an apricot tinge. 'Erfurt' is a rose from a different stable but similar to the hybrid musks and certainly one of the loveliest introductions of Wilhelm Kordes. It makes an arching bush about 1.5 × 1.8m (5 × 6ft) and bears white-centred, rose pink flowers with a boss of golden stamens right throughout the summer.

Some of the modern shrub roses are simply vigorous tall-growing floribundas, such as 'Dorothy Wheatcroft' and 'Fred Loads'. One of the best is 'Chinatown', which grows to about 1.2m (4ft), producing clusters of large, double yellow flowers of exceptionally sweet fragrance. There may be a pause between flushes but it does flower again throughout the summer.

That cannot be said of 'Constance Spry', but it does represent another important development in modern shrub roses, in some of which the style of the old roses has been recaptured. I have not found this as fragrant as others claim it to be, but it is an outstandingly beautiful rose, soft pink and very full. However, a characteristic it unfortunately shares with most of the old roses is that it flowers in mid-summer only. It is a lax grower up to about 1.8m (6ft) and can be grown either as a shrub or as a short climber.

Old Garden Roses

The old garden roses that mercifully, in the new classification have been left much as they were, still hold their fascination. Partly it is a matter of them being a link with the past, historically and horticulturally; partly it is because their beauty and qualities are very different to those of most modern roses. To my way of thinking it is pointless setting the old against the new. We can enjoy them both but to get the best out of old and new roses you will probably find that it is best to avoid putting varieties of one kind close to varieties of the other.

Of the old roses the gallicas are historically among the most important. They are probably the first roses cultivated by man and ancestors of most of the roses that we grow in our gardens. The apothecary's rose, *R. gallica* 'Officinalis' was one of the mainstays of medieval herbalism. It and its sport, 'Rosa Mundi', are typical of this group in their size and habit. They are fairly compact, rarely growing more than 1.2m (4ft) high so that they are among the most suitable of the old roses for the small garden.

The disadvantages of this group, however, are that when growing on their own roots they tend to sucker very freely, and their foliage, which in any case is rather coarse, is often attacked by mildew in late summer.

'Charles de Mills' is a good variety with large rich crimson flowers that are often quartered. The shoots are rather slender so flowers may need some support when they are fully open. 'Rosa Mundi' is after centuries still worth growing as a novelty for its semi-double flowers splashed crimson on a blush-pink background. Because they are only semi-double the flowers do not need the support that those of many gallicas do. It is sometimes recommended as a hedge but I would not advocate this except in a very large garden, for the bush can look scruffy when flowering is over.

The damasks are another very old group of roses but there is no evidence to support the story that they were brought back to Western Europe from the Damascus area by the Crusaders. The autumn damask (*R.* × *damascena semperflorens*), sometimes known as 'Quatre Saisons', was

At Mottisfont Abbey, a property in Hampshire owned by the National Trust, the distinguished plantsman and authority on old roses, Graham Thomas, has laid out the large walled garden to contain the many varieties he has assembled over years of collecting.

Lady's mantle, *Alchemilla mollis*, is one of the most useful herbaceous perennials to combine with roses. It complements perfectly the pure white flowers with green central carpel of the damask rose 'Madame Hardy'.

the sole rose in the West that showed any repeat flowering. By an accidental cross with a China, this variety gave rise to the Bourbons, the first Western group to be remantant.

Of the damasks one of the most outstandingly beautiful is 'Madame Hardy'. It has its faults – on my light soil its performance is rather disappointing – but it can make a shrub up to 1.8m (6ft) high, carrying a mid-summer display of snow-white, flat, quartered flowers with a neat green carpel in the centre. The damasks have a reputation for being strongly scented but the flowers on my own plant of 'Madame Hardy' are not noticeably fragrant. For the small garden, a better damask might be 'Ispahan'. It is reasonably compact, and the loosely double, soft pink flowers are richly scented and carried for six weeks or more.

The Romans almost certainly knew the albas (which, despite their name, are not all white) and they may be responsible for having introduced them to Western Europe. They tend to be large vigorous shrubs, not so easily fitted into the small garden but, where there is the space, invaluable because they will thrive even in a cold position against a north-facing wall. The lovely grey-green foliage is the perfect complement to the white or soft pink flowers.

'Great Maiden's Blush' and 'Maiden's Blush' are very similar roses, growing to about 1.8m (6ft), although the latter is marginally shorter and the flowers have fewer petals. The soft pink, sweetly scented flowers are wonderfully delicate. 'Félicité Parmentier', which makes a shrub of about 1.2 × 1.2m (4 × 4ft), is one Alba that can be fitted into almost any garden. It is unusual in that the blush-pink flowers open from yellow buds.

The Centifolias and Moss Roses

The centifolias (the original cabbage roses) and the moss roses can be considered as one group for we do know that the first moss rose was simply a sport of a centifolia. The origin of the centifolias is obscure but they have long been popular, as the record of seventeenth and eighteenth century Dutch painting shows. These roses need careful positioning in the garden for the stems tend to be very lax and are easily weighed down by the many-petalled flowers.

Fortunately, there is a reasonably upright, small centifolia that can be fitted into even a very small garden. 'De Meaux' is not likely to reach

1.2m (4ft) and its sweetly scented, soft pink flowers will only cause the canes to arch gently so that there isn't a need to stake the bush. The exquisitely beautiful 'Fantin Latour' is another reasonably sturdy, upright variety but as it grows to 2m (7ft) it is not a shrub for the small garden. The many-petalled flowers are soft pink and when they reflex they sometimes show a button eye.

Of the moss roses 'Henri Martin' is useful for having light crimson flowers, which can make a good contrast to some of the paler old roses. It grows to about 1.5m (5ft), making a very thorny bush but the moss can be rather sparse. A much more heavily mossed variety – and one that is also very thorny – is 'William Lobb'. The double flowers are dark purple with a magenta reverse; after a day or so they fade to an equally beautiful soft lilac. This is a very vigorous grower, probably best used as a short climber.

The first China roses reached Europe in the middle of the eighteenth century. The process of deliberate crossing was not then understood so that, despite their repeat-flowering habit, these cultivated varieties were not exploited as breeding material. Later, roses such as 'Old Blush' did pass on their flowering habit. 'Old Blush' is still an attractive garden plant, growing to about 90cm (3ft) and producing its pale-pink double flowers over a long period – sometimes still to Christmas time.

It was the chance crossing of China and European roses at the beginning of the nineteenth century that led to the development of vigorous, repeat-flowering varieties from which the modern bush roses are derived. Some of the Bourbons and Portland roses, the first phase in this development, are still very beautiful and desirable roses.

'Madame Isaac Pereire' is a Bourbon with exceptionally fragrant flowers; some say it is the most strongly scented of all roses. It can be a robust grower, reaching a height of 2m (7ft), but it is worth growing not only for its scent but also for the sumptuous beauty of fully double, globular flowers of a deep cerise-pink. A more delicately beautiful Bourbon is 'La Reine Victoria', a rather lax plant that may need some support. The well-scented globular flowers are very refined, opening pale pink and deepening on exposure to sunlight.

The Bourbons have survived better than the Portlands but one at least of these is still a good plant for a small garden. 'Comte de Chambord' grows to about 1.2m (4ft) and produces a good continuity of deep pink fragrant flowers.

Hybrid Perpetuals
The last of the old roses and the immediate precursors of the hybrid teas are the hybrid perpetuals. These were developed mainly in France and were the result of crossing the Bourbons and, to some extent, the Portland roses, with China roses and later the rather tender tea roses. The vigorous and reasonably repeat-flowering varieties that were produced mainly in France were very popular even though they were not always easy plants to grow (very often the only satisfactory way of dealing with their unusually long stems was to arch them over and peg them down).

Of the hundreds put on the market only a few survive. One with enormous flowers is 'Paul Neyron', with deep pink blooms that can be as much as 15cm (6in) across. A more refined plant is 'Mrs John Laing', which has high-centred, silver-pink flowers and is one of the most recurrent of the hybrid perpetuals. They hint at the way the hybrid teas were eventually to go.

Climbers and Ramblers

The varieties that I have dealt with so far have been bush and shrub roses in the main. I would like to touch briefly on the climbers and ramblers for they do offer the opportunity of getting flower colour at a good height. The climbers are very much a mixed bag but, in general, you can expect them to have small clusters of reasonably large flowers. The newer varieties tend to be recurrent but those that are sports of bush roses do not normally flower as freely as the originals and sometimes they are not recurrent.

I would place 'Aloha' as one of the best climbers of moderate vigour. It will take its time to reach 3m (10ft) (it can be grown quite satisfactorily as a shrub) but it is very healthy and its fragrant flowers, rather in the old style, are a lovely rich pink. After the first flush there will be a pause but this really is a repeat-flowering climber and the second performance will be good.

Another reliable repeat-flowering climber is 'Golden Showers', an almost thornless rose with bright yellow but almost scentless flowers. This has a great advantage over many climbers in that, even when it is not trained, as climbing roses should be, along horizontal wires, it will flower low down.

One of the first of the recurrent climbers, 'New Dawn', is still one of the best of those that are moderately vigorous and it has figured prominently in the breeding of new varieties. Though not as resistant to mildew as some of the more recent varieties, it is valuable for its first profuse flowering and the continuity of its beautiful pearly pink, lightly fragrant flowers.

For the gardener who has the space, some of the climbers with only a single flowering season are still worth considering. One of the most sumptuous is 'Madame Grégoire Staechelin' ('Spanish Beauty'). The early summer display of scented pink flowers with ruffled petals is quite breathtaking when covering a wall.

'Madame Alfred Carrière' is another climber making a magnificent early display. This will produce the odd flower later on but it is the first flush of scented creamy flowers that is its glory. This is a vigorous grower, capable of reaching 7.5m (25ft) and will do well even on a north-facing wall.

The ramblers have only one flowering period, which begins about midsummer. The typical rambler has thin, flexible canes that are much easier to train than those of climbers and the flowers are small and borne in large trusses. Some ramblers are very close to the wild climbing roses and some show amazing vigour. They are not plants that are easy to accommodate in a small garden but where there is space and they can be grown over a pergola or similar structure, even into an old tree, they can be very impressive indeed.

The classic example of a vigorous rambler is R. *filipes* 'Kiftsgate'. This

Repeat-flowering climbers are the most suitable roses for training up garden arches. The vigorous but once-flowering ramblers may need the more substantial support of a pergola.

gloriously fragrant rose produces immense heads of single, creamy-white flowers but it can extend much more than 9m (30ft) and could overwhelm a small garden. 'Seagull' is a less vigorous but very beautiful rambler growing to a height of about 4m (12ft) that would be more appropriate on the pergola of a modest-sized garden. Its single or semi-double white flowers are larger than those of many ramblers. Another of similar vigour is 'Félicité and Perpétue', another hardy and healthy variety with blush-white pompon flowers that are borne very freely. If you are looking for other colours, consider 'Goldfinch', a strongly scented pale yellow variety that is not likely to make more than 3m (10ft), and 'François Juranville', a vigorous rambler growing to about 7.5m (25ft) and carrying beautiful spicy scented, rose-pink flowers in mid-summer.

Other Roses

In such a brief survey of garden roses it is inevitable that I will have left gaps. I am aware, for instance, of neglecting the miniature roses, which are becoming increasingly popular in Britain, although the interest here is still much more restrained than it is in America. I should say that, although they can be attractive little plants, much of the miniature quality has been lost by crossing them with the floribundas in order to get a wider colour range. The best of them can be very attractively grown in raised beds so that you can see them close at hand and appreciate their qualities for what they are. They are not, as many people mistakenly believe, houseplants.

Work on the breeding of miniature and other varieties of roses continues a tradition that has given us some of our loveliest garden flowers. But I would like to finish by reminding you of the plants from which all our varieties have come, the 150 or so species roses. We would probably be very unhappy if these were the only roses we could have in our gardens but they include some very interesting plants that have great horticultural value. There is the lovely glaucous foliage and purplish stems of *R. glanca (R. rubrifolia)*, the unusual bottle-shaped hips of *R. moyesii* and the extraordinary monster-like armour, the thorns translucent red when young, of *R. sericea pteracantha*. The keen gardener will not despise the quality of these plants which, in their own way, are a match for the charm of the most voluptuous of the cultivated varieties of rose.

121

Covering the Ground

SUSAN CONDER

As an American, Susan Conder has an especially valuable contribution to make to this book, for she has come to love and appreciate a tradition that it not necessarily her own. In common with other American gardeners who have lived and worked in Britain, she has had to come to terms with the same range of physical problems with which native-born gardeners have to cope. Some Americans who have gardened here have done much more than this – Lanning Roper, the distinguished designer, is an obvious example, as is Major Lawrence Johnston, the creator of the garden at Hidcote Manor in Gloucestershire.

Susan Conder herself settled in England in 1970, when she married the architect Neville Conder, of the Casson-Conder partnership. She studied landscape architecture in London, worked in landscape design and as a planting consultant, and is now a professional writer, specializing in horticultural subjects. Her own English gardening experience is in itself an excellent qualification for writing on ground cover. She is planting consultant for the square which her London flat overlooks, while at her country home in West Sussex she and her husband have gradually made a charming, but manageable, garden from rough meadow and woodland.

In this waterside planting, tough dense-growing perennials suitable for ground cover include hostas and *Euphorbia griffithii* 'Fireglow'. The smouldering red of the euphorbia's flower bracts is intensified by the clear yellow of a hybrid globe flower, a variety of *Trollius × cultorum*.

GROUND COVER, like *nouvelle cuisine* in cooking, has become something of a cult, encouraged in part by the somewhat over-optimistic claims in gardening catalogues and by seductively illustrated articles in Sunday colour supplements. A myth now surrounds ground cover, extolling it as the solution to all gardening problems.

There is nothing miraculous about ground cover. It can be an extremely effective and attractive form of gardening, but it can also fail if people expect too much of it, or give too little in the way of careful plant selection, initial site preparation, aftercare and renewal. To

succeed with ground cover, you must face up to the facts about what it can't do, as well as what it can.

The Nature of Ground Cover

Ground cover can be defined, broadly, as any plant with foliage or stems dense enough to hide the soil beneath it and keep down competition from other less desirable plants such as weeds. A closely planted conifer stand, like those established in the early days of the Forestry Commission for timber crops, qualifies as ground cover; so does the tiny moss-like *Sagina pilifera*. In the largest sense, lawn is ground cover, and so is a dense sward of couch grass. Common usage, however, has qualified this definition, so that ground-cover plants are usually ornamental herbaceous perennials or shrubs, although ferns, biennials and annuals are sometimes used for this purpose. Ground-cover plants should be attractive, reasonably tough and quick growing, and easy to maintain. Because people expect ornamental beauty from ground cover, such rampantly effective natural ground cover as dock and ground elder are automatically excluded from gardens, although the variegated ground elder, *Aegopodium podagraria* 'Variegata', has a small but devoted following .

Beauty is always in the eye of the beholder, though, and what might be considered worthy ground cover to one person may well be perceived as worthless by another. I always remember when a friend – naturalized English but South African by birth – cast her eye dismissively over a large clump of *Zantedeschia aethiopica* 'Crowborough', coaxed into flowering in my small walled garden in Sussex.

'What in the world do you want to grow those for?' she asked. 'In South Africa, they're weeds. They grow everywhere; they're called pig lilies because people dig them up and feed them to pigs.'

Matters of taste are inevitably subjective and often inexplicable. In gardening, the worth of a plant is influenced by rarity value, and the English tend to dismiss as potential ground cover that which is native. There is a long established English tradition, dating from the Tradescants in the seventeenth century, of collecting exotic plants, in the interests of botany and for the beautification of greenhouses and gardens, and for the glory of England.

I once accompanied a head gardener and her employer, the 'queen bee' of the garden committee, while they did the rounds of a large, mature London garden. Blessed with huge plane, ailanthus, robina and lime trees around the perimeter, it also had the consequent problem of root-riddled, shaded and dry earth beneath.

One of the few ground covers that had managed to establish itself was *Hedera helix*. Every time the 'queen bee' saw a wide swathe of ivy, she instructed: 'That will have to come out; it's only ivy.' Other native plants – sweet woodruff (*Galium odoratum*, syn. *Asperula odorata*), and ground ivy (*Glechoma hederacea*, syn. *Nepeta glechoma*) – would have provided successful solutions to the poor growing conditions under trees, but no doubt they would have been similarly dismissed.

Obviously, one would never introduce such invasive ground cover into a tiny garden full of choice treasures, because the former's vigour makes them a rampant menace when conditions are favourable. They would, however, have been ideal in that London garden, and certainly far preferable to depressing bare earth punctuated by unsuitable plants (Japanese hostas and South American fuchsias, in this case) struggling to survive. Whatever their other potential, ground-cover plants are beautiful only if they are growing well. It is often a case of re-assessing one's expectations in the face of gardening reality.

Tastes in garden beauty also change with time and hindsight, and there are some plants that grow too well. *Polygonum cuspidatum*, a particularly rampageous Japanese knotweed, was introduced into England in 1825. Some enthusiast planted it in Thurloe Square, London, where it promptly felt at home. Ever since, vain attempts have been made to eradicate the plant. The late Mr Baker, for many years the superb and much loved gardener to Thurloe Square, annually took a

Many of the hardy geraniums are clump-forming perennials that are highly effective as ground cover. Their attractive foliage would be enough to justify their place in the garden; their flowers, which in some species and hybrids are borne over a long period, are an additional merit. Those of *G. psilostemon*, shown here, are of a startling magenta with a black eye.

flame gun to the young, red, insistent growth. In spite of his efforts, and those of subsequent gardeners, the knotweed still remains, a cautionary reminder the will to survive that certain plants demonstrate.

Essential Beauty

Beauty symbols sometimes get in the way of genuine beauty, and one of the most powerful is a flower. Partly because of their romantic overtones, partly because of their potential for bright colour, flowers have come to epitomize successful gardening.

With ground cover, it is the foliage that does virtually all the work, suppressing weed growth, keeping the soil beneath cool and moist, and as the foliage dies, returning nutrients to the soil. The foliage is also present for far more of the year than the flowers.

Graham Stuart Thomas, in his classic book, *Plants for Ground Cover*, advocated the concept of foliar beauty, and of assessing a potential ground cover first for its leaf form, colour, size and texture before even considering the blossom. This is not as Draconian a philosophy as it seems; many ground–cover plants have flowers that are as lovely as their foliage. Certain roses, rhododendron, iris, heather and day lilies make suitable ground cover, and the acanthus is archetypal good ground cover with its handsome foliage and flowers.

Variegated foliage has become a type of beauty symbol, and both catalogues and the gardening press enthuse over each new variegated cultivar. It is easy to see why: the leaf colours become the visual equivalent of flower colour. On the other hand, the more variegated – ie. the less green – a leaf is, the less vigorous the plant, compared to a non-variegated equivalent. In small spoaces, this may be a bonus. One of the many variegated bugles, for example, would be a safer choice than the rampant species. Then, too, some variegations, like the purple, bronze and yellow of *Ajuga* 'Multicolour' (syn. *A.* 'Rainbow') are very hectic and restless looking.

Ground-cover beauty resides as much in combinations of plants and plant groupings as in the quality of individual plants. A generous clump of *Bergenia cordifolia* is enhanced by a setting of, say *Epimedium* × *rubrum* and the lovely black mondo grass, *Ophiopogon planiscapus* 'Nigrescens'. Not one of these plants is dramatically showy or even floriferous, but together the contrasting foliage creates a pleasing tapestry.

Time Scale

Ground cover has also become synonymous with instant results, though the only truly instant results are achieved by planting them shoulder-to-shoulder. Those who construct the displays of ideal gardens, such as the ones seen at the Royal Horticultural Society Chelsea Show, use vast resources and overplanting so that not a speck of earth, not a weed is visible. A week later, when the Show ends, the plants are unceremoniously dug up, sometimes still in their pots, then sold off or carted away to recover. Overplanting is endurable (for the plants) only in the short term.

In normal gardens and with normal budgets, ground-cover plants are

initially spaced 20cm–3m (8in–10ft) apart, depending on their speed of growth, ultimate size and spread. It usually takes two or three growing seasons for them to mat together. Until that happens, regular weeding, either by hand or hoeing, is vital.

Some ground covers are rapid colonizers and will mat up within a single growing season. One such plant is the prostrate evergreen shrub *Rubus tricolor*, a Chinese relation of the ordinary English bramble. (Its cultivation is due as much to its thornlessness as to its foreignness.) Its heart-shaped, dark-green leaves, bristly stems, single white flowers and occasional red fruit are modestly attractive – rather than beautiful – but it will thrive in dense shade and bone-dry soil. Its annual growth of 1m (3ft) or more can be kept under control by pruning, and the prunings used as cuttings to colonize yet more inhospitable ground. Like other members of the *Rubus* family, it is attractive to wildlife and a good source of nectar for butterflies.

Another quick-growing ground cover tolerant of shade and dry soil is the dwarf bamboo, *Sasa veitchii*, previously and variouly called *Bambusa veitchii*, *Arundinaria veitchii*, *Arundinaria albomarginata* and *Sasa marginata*. It doesn't bear close inspection, with its rough habit of growth and its leaf edges fading to a straw colour towards the end of summer, but it is most effective seen en masse and is, again, far nicer than bare earth or assorted weeds.

Speed is a two-edged sword, though, and involves constant vigilance and pruning back, especially if there is less space available than the plant is ultimately capable of covering. Deterioration of the plant is another potential drawback. As a general rule, the quicker a plant grows (particularly if it is deciduous), the shorter lived it is, relative to others of its type. Of ground-cover shrubs, quick-growing potentillas, brooms and deutzias, for example, are shorter lived than the slow but steady rhododendrons and skimmias.

Of the herbaceous perennial ground covers, variegated dead nettle, *Lamiastrum galeobdolon* 'Variegatum', can arch and loop its way over large

Some of the fastest-growing ground-cover plants need to be treated with considerable caution. In favourable conditions they can spread as vigorously and aggressively as the weeds they are meant to exclude. Many perennials and shrubs will only build up a close ground cover, as here, over a period of several years and until they do the border will need to be weeded.

Lady's mantle, *Alchemilla mollis*, is a ground-covering perennial that self seeds very freely. It is such a beautiful plant, its soft leaves magically holding droplets of water and its lime-green flowers blending so easily with other plants, that most gardeners would be happy to put up with its proliferation.

areas in a single season, sending down roots from every leaf node. By the end of the second season, however, bare patches of soil usually appear, as the plants' energies are dissipated, and ever new ground is colonized. The solution is either to prune it back hard after flowering, or to lift the older plants and replace them with rooted pieces of young growth, after forking over the soil and incorporating a little leaf mould or other fertilizer. Neither of these tasks is difficult or time consuming, but it does dispel the myth of ground cover as a perpetually attractive, maintenance-free plant. Colour photographs in books always show ground cover at its finest, a patchwork of densely interwoven plants carpeting a garden. Such enticing images somehow equate gardening with the process of painting a picture which, once finished, remains in that state indefinitely. More helpful and realistic, perhaps, would be time-lapse photography, showing the initially planted site, and each year thereafter, in winter as well as in the growing season, for the next ten or so years.

I remember seeing an elderly friend's Sussex garden, some years ago, awash with the semi-hardy *Convolvulus mauritanicus*. This low-growing, woody-stemmed relative of the annual morning glory had produced its blue and white, funnel-shaped flowers almost everywhere. Growing from the narrow, south-facing border at the foot of the house walls, the plants had sent stems trailing over the stone terrace and along the cracks in the paving, and outposts of this clear, delightful blue were established in the sandy rock garden that sloped away from the terrace. *Convolvulus mauritanicus* festooned out-of-flower heather and climbed through the lower branches of flowering fuchsias, adding its blue to their pale and deep pinks. This was ground cover rampant in the nicest possible way and a proverbial picture was created.

The following summer, there was not a single *Convolvulus mauritanicus* to be seen. When asked where it was, my friend explained that the bad winter had killed it and that she was trying *Acaena microphylla* instead. (Little plugs of it could be seen evenly spaced, where the ground had previously been occupied by *Convolvulus mauritanicus*). In her mind's eye she had already created a ferny, ground-hugging carpet of blue-green, enlivened with rusty-red burrs. No mourning, no regrets, just an opporunity to try another plant and another visual effect – the mark of a true gardener, and one who understands the nature of ground cover.

Stock Renewal

The uncertainties of weather aside, all plants mature and eventually become over-mature, each according to its own life cycle, and all gardening, including ground-cover gardening, is an ongoing process, like a never-finished canvas. Some perennial plants, such as the evergreen Christmas rose, *Helleborus niger*, slowly increase in girth for many years, and actually resent being lifted and divided. Others, such as heather and pinks, are relatively short-lived, depending on growing conditions, and need renewing after three, four, five, or more years.

Renewing doesn't necessarily mean expenditure. Pinks can be propagated by division and cuttings as well as from ripe seed; and heather can be layered or divided, or cuttings taken. In traditional herbaceous borders, lifting and dividing every three years was the general rule, to prevent natural overcrowding, to discard the older, worn-out centres of plants and to replace them with the stronger, younger outer growth. Many of the most popular ground-cover plants – hostas, heucheras, lady's mantle, iris, nepeta, achillea, sedum and primulas – did generations of service in herbaceous borders. Re-naming them ground-cover plants does not change how they are cultivated!

Self seeding is a natural form of renewal and again, is a two-edged sword. If the ground to be covered is large and otherwise bare of plants, every seedling that appears is a bonus. In a small garden, self-sown seedlings, even of ideal ground-cover plants, are a nuisance. Famous (or infamous) perennial self seeders are lemon balm (*Melissa officinalis*); Siberian bugloss (*Brunnera macrophylla*); mourning widow (*Geranium phaeum*); lady's mantle (*Alchemilla mollis*); and the silvery-white leaved *Lychnis coronaria*. Cowslips (*Primula veris*) seed themselves prolifically in the rough grass under our fruit trees. All of these are ground-cover plants to choose consciously or to avoid, according to the needs of the garden.

Suitable Sites

Ideally, ground-cover plants should be sold bearing a label stating that the plant will act as ground cover only when planted in suitable conditions. Ground-cover plants growing in unsuitable conditions fail to thrive and therefore look unattractive, fail to keep down weeds and are more liable to fall prey to the hosts of insect pests and diseases that are potentially present in even the most immaculate garden. For example, the giant kingcup, *Caltha polypetala*, is ideal ground cover for rich, boggy ground. Here it flowers profusely, spreading its branching, rooting stems 1m (3ft) or more in a single season, and concealing the soil with its huge, round, shiny green leaves. Given a dry sandy spot in a border, the plant fails as ground cover, through no fault of its own. Conversely, growing heathers and rhododendrons, both ideal ground covers in poor sandy, acid soil, in rich waterlogged heavy soil is equally doomed.

These are extreme examples, and there are certain ground covers which are tolerant of a wide range of conditions. *Iris sibirica*, for example, *Alchemilla mollis* and most hostas are equally happy in damp and dry soil. In my garden, clumps of *Hosta sieboldii* grow at the foot of a hornbeam hedge, in sandy, lean soil and with the hornbeam's roots competing for water and the hornbeam itself creating rain shade. Clumps of *Hosta sieboldii* also grow in the artificial bog garden, in which the soil is heavily enriched with compost, and kept moist by the overflow of the adjacent artificial pond (fed rainwater from a pipe linked to the roof downpipe).

The hostas in the bog grow bigger than those under the hornbeam hedge, but the luxurious foliage of the former tends to be more attractive to slugs, so that by the end of summer, the leaves are usually reduced to perforated fragments.

Potential Enemies

In terms of resilience and regeneration, plants that sucker, layer, root from leaf nodes or have many growth points are better as ground cover – especially in heavily used gardens – than those that grow from a single

Hard surfaces can seem very hard until they are softened by vegetation. Short-growing plants that root as they go are ideal for growing between slabs of paving. The ivies are especially good at making a living in quite dry shady conditions, where many other plants will not thrive.

point. Stepping on the prostrate snowberry, *Symphoricarpos × chenaultii* 'Hancock', does little long-term damage and may even encourage more suckering. Stepping on the main stem of, say, *Viburnum davidii* or *Prunus laurocerasus* 'Zabeliana' causes a major, if not fatal, setback.

With the English, dogs and children are potential enemies of ground-cover plants. In some London squares, the canine population is disproportionately high, due to lack of private gardens and the large number of flats. On the child front, the slow but steady demise of the English nanny has allowed unsupervised children almost complete freedom of action playing outdoors. Both dogs and children establish 'runs' through shrubberies and mixed planting. Large woody or thorny shrubs, such as the lovely bluish-white stemmed bramble, *Rubus cockburnianus*, are bypassed, but smaller ground cover is inevitably trampled. As well as physical damage caused to the plants, such 'runs' have very compacted soil, impenetrable by water or plant roots.

In addition, children like to create hidden dens or camps in dense planting, clearing away any inconvenient (to them) foliage nearby. Children are also keen hoarders and highly imaginative. Some years ago one little girl stripped the north end of Thurloe Square of hundreds of daffodils, which she said, were for making perfume (ironically, most were unscented). The steely blue thistles of *Echinops ritro* are often snapped off and used by small boys to bombard each other, an unorthodox but effective way of spreading this excellent ground cover, provided the seeds heads are mature.

Dogs, like children, are destructive of ground cover, but not wilfully so. Bitch urine can cause foliage and patches of lawn to turn brown. (The turf usually recovers after a month or so, although the chemicals favour the growth of coarse, not fine, grass). Male dogs mark out their territory with urine, applying a little at a time to several places, and choosing the same places (and plants) over and over again. Asking any ground-cover plant to survive in such conditions is unreasonable.

Fencing ground cover to protect it from such ravages is usually unsuccessful. Permanent fencing is expensive; temporary fencing, such as wire mesh or chestnut paling, looks nasty, thus defeating one of the primary purposes of ground cover.

In suburban and rural areas, deer and rabbits are additional hazards to ground cover, especially in bad winters and late springs. Adequate fencing against deer needs to be at least 1.8m (6ft) high and though rabbit fencing is lower, it must also continue below ground, or splay out at ground level, to prevent burrowing. (Rabbit fencing is not a serious obstacle to hares.)

Unless your garden is totally private, enclosed, fortified, childless and dogless, you must accept that a certain amount of healthy plant fall-out is inevitable, and that replacement and replanting is part of the nature of gardening.

Even then, nature provides additional challenge. The most fearsome is the killer disease caused by honey fungus, *Armillaria mellea*. The fungus is sometimes called bootlace fungus because of the bootlace-like rhizomorphs that travel through the soil from the point of infection – usually a rotten tree stump, on which the honey-coloured mushrooms can be seen in late summer and autumn – to the victim plant. The fungus is usually associated with broadleaved trees, and the rhizomorphs can travel many many metres from the original source. It attacks a wide range of woody plants and some herbaceous perennials, and can occur in urban gardens as well as rural ones. Some ground-cover plants, including ivy, laurel, holly and mahonia, are thought to be more resistant than others, such as privet and rhododendron.

There is no known permanent cure. Although fungicides and soil sterilants may give temporary relief – it is vital to dig up and burn infected plants – ground can become reinfected, particularly if the source of infection remains intact.

Some gardeners go to the vast effort and expense of digging out and replacing areas of infected soil with fresh, or digging two spits deep over the infected site, sterilizing the soil and replanting with reputedly disease-resistant species six months later.

In our case, after trying to control an outbreak of honey fungus by soil sterilization and finding heartbreaking evidence of re-infection, we built a pond and PVC-lined bog garden, neither of which comes into direct contact with the infected soil, and laid brick terraces over the surrounding suspect area. Plants now grow there in pots and tubs, in no danger of infection and enjoying the reflected heat of the brick.

The ultimate English response to honey fungus is polite but total defiance, and it sometimes works. Two country gardening friends of mine discovered honey fungus in their gardens, burned the infected plant material, and immediately re-planted the untreated spot with the same species. In both cases, so far, there has been no recurrence of the disease.

Planting and Nurturing

How you plant ground cover affects its future as much as the initial choice of plants. The soil has to be open in texture, so air and water can reach the roots. This means, especially in the case of old, worn-out soil in town gardens, digging over the soil, or at least forking it over, and incorporating well-rooted leaf mould, compost, or peat.

Though seemingly contradictory, the plant also has to be very firmly planted, so its roots come into definite contact with the soil to provide anchorage and take in nutrients and water. The worst approach is to gouge a hole out of rock-like, compacted soil, then jam in the plant and hope for the best. Always make the planting hole generously larger than the root ball. If the surrounding soil is poor, back-fill with a mixture of soil-based compost and peat or well-rotted compost or leaf mould. Use your fist, your feet or the back of a trowel to firm the soil immediately round the plant. Test for firmness afterwards by giving a strong tug at the base (not a leaf, which will simply tear off); if it moves, re-plant it.

The optimum size of material for planting depends on the growing conditions. A well-grown containerized *Vinca major*, for example, could be immediately broken into three or four separate portions, each with a few roots and trailing stems. Given weed-free, reasonably good soil, sufficient water, and the absence of human and animal interference, the small portions could produce more verdure in one season than the

single, large plant. Given less than ideal conditions, it is safer to leave the plant intact, to increase its chance of establishment and survival, before worrying about propagation.

Lack of water, in the spring and autumn as well as summer months, is the greatest enemy of newly planted ground cover. This is especially true of ground cover shaded by trees, whose crowns act as umbrellas and whose roots consume enormous quantities of water. It is pointless watering on compacted soil, as the water rolls off the surface. Fork over the surrounding soil beforehand, so the water can percolate downwards.

It is possible to orchestrate ground-cover plants with varying life cycles so that short-lived, relatively expendible ornamental plants cover the ground while the slower-growing ones become established, and weeds have no room to grow. In sheltered gardens, for example, the 'Headbourne Hybrids' of *Agapanthus* make admirable ground cover, but are relatively expensive and slow to become established. Interplanting them with the quicker growing *Ajuga reptans* or the lovely alpine strawberry, *Fragaria vesca*, provides attractive ground cover which can gradually be removed and used elsewhere or given away, as the *Agapanthus* take hold. Remember to provide sufficient water and nutrients for both. Theoretically, the long-term ground cover would grow more quickly given no competition at all, but bare earth is always an anathema to a ground-cover gardener, and compromise, however unorthodox, the *modus operandi*.

The strap-shaped leaves of *Agapanthus* Headbourne Hybrids eventually form dense ground cover but clumps are slow to build up and they will need to be interplanted with expendable plants until they become established. Here they are growing in the Savill Garden in Windsor Great Park, Berkshire, a garden of exceptional quality created by Sir Eric Savill in the 1930s.

133

Cottage Garden Medley

ANNE SCOTT-JAMES

Anne Scott-James – in her own words, 'one of nature's cottage gardeners' – has made and tended the traditional garden that surrounds her cottage on the Berkshire Downs for almost fifty years. Her enthusiasm for her subject is made abundantly clear in everything she says and writes, proving the point that devoted amateur gardeners, such as Miss Scott-James, are the real makers of the English garden tradition – though few are as wittily instructive.

Two of Miss Scott-James' books, *Down to Earth* and *The Cottage Garden* are really essential reading for all amateur gardeners, the first being particularly good reference for those interested in the modern style of cottage garden, the subject she and I have chosen to concentrate on here. For a fascinating account of the history of these simple, but inspiring, gardens, turn to the second book and you will not be disappointed.

Miss Scott-James is as gifted as an interviewer as she is as a writer, so it was with some trepidation that I embarked on the task of turning her words into prose. What follows is an appetiser, rather than a main course. Take it as a starting point and go to her books. You will not be disappointed.

One of the finest twentieth-century gardens inspired by the cottage tradition is at Sissinghurst Castle in Kent. Here Vita Sackville-West and her husband Sir Harold Nicolson imposed a degree of symmetry on an irregular plot through the creation of a number of small interconnected gardens. The cottage, one of several scattered buildings, is surrounded by flowers in warm tones.

SOME PEOPLE NOW CLAIM that the pretty cottage garden, stocked with old-fashioned flowers, herbs, vegetables and fruit, is a Victorian invention, a sentimental fiction fixed in the mind's eye by charming painters like Helen Allingham, who saw rural life *en couleur de rose*. I do not believe this. There is a good deal of evidence that cottage gardens, with plenty of vegetables and herbs, some fruit and flowers, animated by poultry and bees, were cultivated hundreds of years ago by quite simple country people such as small farmers and village craftsmen, and, of course, their wives. If the cottage garden was later elevated to an idyll and developed by the rich into a grander form, it did not begin that

way. It has its roots in the ancient need for rural people to eke out their wretched wages by growing their own produce.

There can be no doubt, however, that this simple tradition has been a powerful influence on gardeners working with much greater resources than were ever available to the ordinary cottager. Gertrude Jekyll, for example, one of the most influential figures in twentieth-century gardening, considered that she gardened in a cottage style even though she was accustomed to a scale of several acres and the help of trained staff. Other influential gardeners, too, have found inspiration in English cottage gardens, the best known being Vita Sackville-West and her husband, Harold Nicolson, creators of the garden at Sissinghurst Castle, in Kent. It was Vita Sackville-West who described another great

The first cottage gardens were simple collections of herbs and vegetables for feeding very hungry people. A vegetable plot and a herb bed still feature in any cottage garden worthy of the name.

twentieth-century garden, Hidcote Manor, as 'a cottage garden on the most glorified scale'.

At a less exalted level there are many who consider themselves, as I do, to be cottage gardeners. Not for us the grand effects of the formal garden. We would not know where to begin if we had to subordinate our chief pleasure in gardening – our personal bond with a jostling crowd of plants – to a severely rational scheme of landscaping or husbandry. Our enthusiasms include the cultivation of rare alpines, weekend self-sufficiency and the conservation of native plants. We have in common our love of plants and a feeling for tradition sufficient to keep the cottage garden flourishing.

Cottage Gardens of the Past

When you ask about the way that tradition began it has to be admitted that information is very scanty. But we can be certain that the first cottage gardens were totally useful, producing food for very hungry people. The 'fortunate' cottager probably had no more than a fenced-in yard with a few animals and poultry and, protected from these by simple wattle hurdles, a patch of vegetables and herbs. The range of vegetables that were grown probably did not go much beyond beans, cabbage, leeks and onions. Most herbs were probably picked wild but some were certainly grown, although perhaps less for flavouring than for medicinal purposes. The most fortunate cottagers may have had a fruit tree and beehives.

Even with a limited and essentially practical range of plants, a garden could look quite picturesque; herbs can be very pretty and so can a hawthorn hedge. However, it was probably not until the sixteenth century that the cottage garden began to be ornamental. Some of the enthusiasm for gardening, new crops and improved flowers shown by the Elizabethan upper classes must have rubbed off on the cottager. I have never believed that the poor even in very poor times were insensate. A homely book of verse, Thomas Tusser's *A Hundred Points of Good Husbandry* of 1557 – which was later expanded to *Five Hundred Points* and appeared in numerous editions – gives some idea of how a small farmer and his wife managed their land. The garden, as distinct from the farm and orchard, was the dominion of the housewife. We don't get much sense of the gardening style other than hints of the profuse mingling that we now think of as typically cottagey. There is, however, mention of numerous vegetables, herbs and fruits, including pompions (pumpkins) and rounceval peas to boil and butter, violets to add to salads, lavender and tansy for strewing, hops and strawberries for stilling and rhubarb for physic. Among the forty or so flowers suggested for purely decorative use, many would have been unimproved wild flowers. There are references to columbines, double marigolds, hollyhocks, lilies, nigella, peonies, roses, snapdragons and sweet williams, all of which are still mainstays of the cottage garden.

When we read the early-seventeenth-century authorities on plants and husbandry, particularly John Parkinson, author of *Paradisi in Sole, Paradisus Terrestris*, we really feel that the cottage garden has come into focus and that the pattern which has survived down to our own day is firmly established. This is only partly true – the erratic prosperity of humble cottagers has given the tradition many hiccoughs. In good times the poor may have taken the gardens of yeomen farmers, or even of gentry, as models for their own little patches and grown plants not only to eat but also for the delight of cultivating beautiful flowers. The gardener at the big house or the lord of the manor might pass on a choice plant, a cutting or a bulb. In the first half of the nineteenth century many landowners were persuaded by the crusading zeal of reformers such as John Claudius Loudon to improve the living conditions of their tenants.

The old style of cottage garden, consisting of a mixture of simple and useful plants, reached its zenith in about 1860. The style has never completely vanished but as the century wore on cottage gardening lost some of its spontaneity, the charmingly romantic effect being achieved by design rather than through artlessness.

The romantic cult of simple country life owes much to the eighteenth-century philosopher Jean-Jacques Rousseau. His influence can be detected in the ideals of the ladies of Llangollen, who ran away together from aristocratic homes in Ireland and in 1780 took a cottage in Wales, where they achieved celebrity leading a life of retirement dedicated to friendship, study and the arts. Visitors described their little property as a cottage garden. Its strictly useful aspects, the vegetables and fruit, and the livestock, always held a place of honour. Furthermore, within their enclosures they grew wild flowers such as primroses and violets. But their gardening was exquisitely refined: the planting included choice new varieties and the work was mainly carried out by gardeners and labourers. The garden of the ladies of Llangollen is a long way from the simple patch of the tenant farmer or labourer.

However, the romantic strand is an increasingly important element in the history of the cottage garden. Sometimes, as in the Wordsworths' garden at Dove Cottage, Grasmere, the romantic and the useful were nicely balanced. Dorothy's journal reveals that the garden was managed with great love and care, admittedly with some paid help, though William and his sister did a lot of the practical work themselves.

Perhaps most importantly in terms of the development of gardens, the romantic view of the cottage garden led to a renewed appreciation of the plants long associated with it and a reaction to the lavish formality that was fashionable in the Victorian period. In one of the most influential of all gardening books, *The English Flower Garden*, first published in 1883, William Robinson praises the simplicity of the English cottage garden, finding the secret of its charm in 'the absence of any pretentious "plan"'. The Edwardians took Robinson's advice to heart. The luxuriant herbaceous planting in the gardens of the well-to-do, particularly in those designed by Miss Gertrude Jekyll, were inspired directly by old cottage borders, although on a much grander scale than was ever originally conceived.

Cottage gardens today

In our modern gardens we have had to abandon the most labour intensive features, such as the herbaceous borders, so loved by the

Edwardians. Perhaps by gardening on a more modest scale we come closer to the spirit of the old cottage gardens. But, like gardeners of other periods, we have our own fashions even when we are not aware of the trends we set or follow.

I cannot put forward my own garden as a model for the modern cottage garden, because, in recent years, I have had to sacrifice plants which are labour intensive. In its glorious past, when I was younger, stronger and healthier, I grew masses of vegetables, without which a cottage garden is not worthy of the name. Today my knees are too creaky to endure much stooping and, of edible plants, I can only manage herbs. It does, however, represent a very large category- the weekend garden. Working it and enjoying it for nearly fifty years has taught me a lot about the problems of making and maintaining a cottage garden that will be untended a lot of the time. I also have a memory well stocked with the successes that other more accomplished gardeners have achieved.

Basic structure

As a starting point I strongly recommend a simple structure. The typical layout of old cottage gardens conformed to one of two groundplans. In the first, a cottage was set back from a road and the

In a classic cottage garden plan the narrow strip separating the cottage from a road or lane was planted with ornamentals and climbers – in particular roses and honeysuckle – while the main garden of vegetables and herbs lay behind.

straight path leading to the main door was bordered with flowers, behind which vegetables were grown in rows. Wherever possible, the privy and muck-heap were tucked out of the way behind the cottage. In an equally typical ground-plan, a cottage might be built close to a road or lane, with the main garden devoted largely to vegetables and fruit behind. A small front garden, separated from the road or lane by a fence or hedge, would be used for growing flowers. These classic ground-plans and their many variations can still be found everywhere in England.

Few gardeners start with an ideal site and, in any case, there can hardly be rules for designing something as informal as a cottage garden, but a strong central axis makes a bold, welcoming opening. Changes of level, even quite modest ones on a flat or almost flat site, can save a garden from being dull. To get an effect of mystery or surprise some of the garden should be concealed. The creation of separate enclosures can be the salvation of a garden on a difficult, irregular site. Hidcote Manor is an outstanding example of a garden on the grand scale that consists of separate, and delightfully varied enclosures. On a regular site some of the garden's effect can be held back by planting within a series of bays formed by hedges and shrubs so that to discover the garden you have to walk down the full length of the main path.

In the traditional cottage garden there are no planned colour schemes, but there is close planting, especially of sweetly scented flowers. The combination here includes tobacco flowers and lilies.

As for the paths, I suggest using the very best materials you can afford. My own garden is far from labour-saving as I have grass paths. Mown grass makes a lovely finish to a garden but, if I did not have a man to do the mowing, I would have paths of brick, cobbles or stone, laid in traditional patterns so that there would be the bonus of lovely texture.

Luxuriant Planting

As came out in our preliminary discussion, there is no such thing as a typical modern cottage garden but a feature that all the most successful share is luxuriant planting. Nearly all of those whom I regard as authorities recommend close planting. Mrs Margery Fish, for example, who brought together a wonderfully harmonious cottage mixture at East Lambrook Manor, in Somerset, was quite firm that you should ignore the standard advice on planting distances: 'Plants are happy in close company, plant much more thickly than they tell you in the books'.

To plant closely you must begin with beds that are well prepared and manured. In the old cottage gardens the muck-heap of garden refuse and slops was supplemented with ashes and chimney soot, pig's dung and night-soil from the privy. When indoor plumbing did away with the privy the garden lost one of its most important traditional sources of fertility. However, almost any household has enough refuse to make a compost heap into a valuable alternative source of organic material.

The now common use of mulches, ranging from compost to peat and pulverized bark, might surprise the old cottage gardeners. For the modern gardener they represent a great saving in labour, for they help to hold moisture in the soil and, provided that they are laid in a thick layer, they suppress weeds.

Authentic old flowers

Since the end of the eighteenth century, plants have been introduced to our gardens from other parts of the temperate world in such numbers and so successfully that it is difficult to know what the authentic old cottage flowers are. To get the accurate idea, you want to go back to early pundits like Thomas Tusser or to authors like Miss Mitford of Three Mile Cross, whose book *Our Village*, written between 1824 and 1832, gives a detailed picture based on Hampshire villages that she knew well.

Many of the flowers the old authorities mention are simply beautiful and useful hardy perennial plants taken from woods and fields. Among the best loved are the cowslip, primrose and violet. As Mrs Fish says, 'No other flower seems quite so much at home in the cottage garden as does the primrose'. In the Middle Ages it was used in cooking; like many flowers, it worked its passage by being useful and decorative. We think of the violet as a posy flower but for centuries it had many uses. As a strewing herb it was supposed to discourage fleas; it was woven into garlands; it was a welcome addition to stuffings, sauces and salads, and as a syrup or paste it was highly valued as a medicament.

Double flowers are rather unfashionable at the moment but in the old cottage gardens they were very much treasured. It is not difficult to imagine how exciting something new and different might be if you were gardening with a relatively limited range of plants. A double marsh marigold or hose-in-hose cowslips must have had a value to the early cottage gardeners even greater than that which new introductions have for us.

Some of the flowers mentioned at a very early date that we now think of as quintessential cottage plants were certainly introductions. The madonna or cottage lily (*Lilium candidum*) is a native of the eastern Mediterranean but it has been grown in Britain since about 1400 at least. Perhaps because it is happiest in a permanent planting, it often does very much better in simple cottage gardens than it does if planted in a more sophisticated setting.

The crown imperial is another relatively early introduction. John Parkinson wrote about it in 1629, praising 'its stately beautifulness'. Mrs Ewing, who in the late nineteenth century founded a Parkinson Society 'to search out and cultivate old flowers which have become scarce', mentions it as surviving chiefly in cottage gardens, as does Mrs Fish more than seventy-five years later.

The one stately plant that from 1850 features in nearly every painting of a cottage garden is the oriental hollyhock (*Althaea rosea*) but it is a genuinely early introduction, probably coming to Britain in 1573.

Beekeeping, one of the oldest of the cottager's skills, almost certainly encouraged the growing of good nectar and pollen plants even though bees forage well beyond the vicinity of their hives to get an adequate supply of food. Lavender, such a traditional plant by the cottage door that it is often thought of as a native, is an introduction from the Mediterranean region but it has been well-established in Britain since the Middle Ages. Much more than a good bee plant, it makes one of the best scented herbs for drying and in the Elizabethan period was commonly used for strewing. Other good bee plants include borage, mignonette, scabious and thyme. A later introduction is *Limnanthes douglasii*, a popular North American species that first reached Britain in 1833.

In the old cottage gardens, scented flowers were particularly prized, another reason for growing plants such as mignonette that bees love to work. Mignonette was a favourite of the Victorians but in the Elizabethan period the clove-scented pinks, or gilliflowers, were especially popular. John Parkinson grew twenty-nine different varieties and John Rea, writing some thirty odd years later, had three times that number.

In the late eighteenth century pinks became out of the accepted florists' flowers. In its early meaning, a florist was not someone arranging and selling flowers but a flower breeder who aimed to produce blooms of great size and perfect shape. Little space was needed for the intensive cultivation of prize plants and floristry became a important competitive hobby among cottagers and artisans. Selection and, in the nineteenth century, deliberate hybridization produced an enormous catalogue of varieties, which were shown at exhibitions organized by florists' clubs. By the end of the eighteenth century the number of florists' flowers recognized by specialists was reduced to eight: anemone, auricula, carnation, hyacinth, pink, polyanthus, ranunculus and tulip. But later this list was expanded, taking in tender plants such as dahlias and pelargoniums.

The peak of floristry was in the mid-nineteenth century. In its slow decline all except a small proportion of the varieties so lovingly raised and cherished by artisans and cottagers have been lost. Some that do survive, such as the old laced polyanthus, have come back into favour and are being cultivated by enthusiasts.

Roses and Climbers

Two other broad categories of ornamental plants featured in almost every traditional cottage garden: roses and climbers. The first cottage roses were simply taken from the hedgerow but by the nineteenth century the cabbage roses, the wonderfully full centifolias first developed by Dutch breeders in the seventeenth century, became the cottage speciality. It was for forgotten varieties of these and other old roses that Gertrude Jekyll searched old gardens. 'Dorothy Perkins', the vigorous bright pink rambler that is widely grown and often thought of as a typically old-fashioned cottage plant is a relatively recent introduction, dating from the beginning of this century.

Close planting was one factor giving the cottage garden a luxuriant effect. Another was the very free use of climbing plants against cottage walls, around the porch or to create an arbour. Rivalling the rose for pride of place is the honeysuckle, or woodbine. Other plants that were used were clematis, convolvulus, everlasting pea, ivy, jasmine and passion-flower.

More surprising, is the importance given to vines or wall-grapes. In the nineteenth century at least two dozen varieties were perfectly

The authentic cottage flowers speak with an uncomplicated directness that is often absent in showy cultivars and exotics. This closely-packed bed of spring flowers includes cowslips and the elegant old-fashioned polyanthus.

hardy in the south of the country and were commonly grown as highly ornamental and productive plants.

Fruit trees, too, were often grown against cottage walls; one occasionally still sees a vestige of this in an ancient pear tree grown as an espalier. In his scheme for planting a plot of an eighth of an acre (an ideal unit, in his view, to feed a family of five), John Claudius Loudon omitted standard fruit-trees. He considered that valuable space could be saved by training fruit – including currants and gooseberries as well as apples, cherries and pears – against the house.

Species versus Cultivars

Like many other gardeners with a marked preference for the informal luxuriance of the cottage garden, I don't choose to grow its traditional flowers to the exclusion of everything else. This is partly because I have a garden that is too big for me, partly a matter of having to find labour-saving solutions. But it is also because there are many other beautiful plants which do not look out of place when grown in a cottagey style.

One clear trend that suits the cottage garden is the greatly increased interest in species, as opposed to highly developed cultivars. An awareness of conservation issues and perhaps a shift in taste in favour of the unostentatious both play a part in this. Among the conservation gardens I know, that of the landscape designer John Codrington is outstanding. There are many native wild plants naturalized in woodland or grass, for John Codrington is anxious to preserve, and to distribute among friends, as much as he can of the increasingly threatened English flora. In addition, there are hundreds of foreign species, reminders of his extensive travels, and proof of his great skill as a plantsman.

144

Shrubs versus Perennials

Another trend, it might be more sensible to speak of it as the general practice, is the planting of shrubs at the expense of herbaceous perennials. The old cottage gardens may have had a flowering shrub such as lilac or myrtle, perhaps an arbour cut out of yew or privet, and a boundary hedge of quickthorn. But the main planting was of hardy herbaceous perennials and the sub-shrubby herbs. The same was true of the cottage-inspired gardens created by William Robinson and Miss Gertrude Jekyll. In the modern garden the most important plants are shrubs. Once established, they do not take as much time to look after as herbaceous plants do. Some are evergreen, and many have attractive foliage as well as flowers. They are far from being the last resort of the despairing gardener but they do need to be used with discretion if they are to make a happy combination with herbaceous plants.

The greatly increased range of foliage plants can also be exploited by the modern cottage gardener. In addition to many fine shrubs with interesting leaves, there is a wide choice of herbaceous plants which are of interest predominantly for their leaves, linear and arching like the grasses, boldly shaped like those of the ornamental rhubarbs and infinitely varied in colouring.

Bold claims have been made for ground-cover plants which might persuade you that these are the ultimate answer for thick planting. I have learned to treat them with great caution. When they are sufficiently vigorous to suppress weeds, their rampant growth can easily smother choice small plants and they can prove very difficult to control. That said, I wouldn't want to be without some of the less aggressive fillers. I particularly like *Alchemilla mollis*, astrantia, the epimediums, many of the geraniums and *Pulmonaria saccharata*.

Alarm at the damage to the environment and the loss of wild plants has focused interest on the species plants that look so much at home in the cottage garden. Honesty and forget-me-not naturalize easily and go well with spring bulbs.

Interest Through the Year

One really worthwhile improvement to make on the old cottage garden is to choose plants that have an extended season in flower, are repeat-flowering or in some other way (for example, good foliage colour or berries in autumn) give a long season of interest. Roses are a case in point. A disadvantage of the old varieties is that most flower only once in the year (although that flowering may be supremely beautiful) whereas many of the modern roses have two good flushes in the year and some flower almost without interruption throughout the summer and into autumn. For the small garden, repeat-flowering roses that are elegant in form and colour and have inherited the old rose fragrance are worth seeking out; there are many of such merit. To get an idea of how a mature plant performs, visit a good rose collection during the flowering season.

Another way to extend the interest of your garden is to plant for autumn, winter and early spring as well as for the peak times of the year. It is something I have done in my own garden so I know well the intense pleasure of coming upon a little clump of cyclamen on a misty autumn morning or finding the blood-red flowers of my earliest hellebore, *H. atrorubens*, on New Year's Day, or spotting the bright blue of *Iris histrioides* 'Major' against the snow in bitter February weather. The flowers that brave the coldest days of the year are as hardy as we could want and almost all have the simple, straightforward beauty of wild plants.

Vegetables and Herbs

You are right to remind me that many modern gardeners in the cottage style want to grow herbs and vegetables as well as ornamental plants. The renewed interest in vegetable growing may have an economic motive – produce is very expensive to buy in the shops – but there are other considerations as well. You know and can control the chemicals and fertilizers you use for your own crops. You can pick the crops and eat them fresh, and in times of glut you can put them in a deep freeze that will keep them in better condition than almost anything you are likely to be able to buy.

Not all converts to vegetable growing have stood the pace. It can be physically demanding, particularly if you garden on heavy soil. And for worthwhile results you have got to keep at it. A really well-cultivated vegetable garden is a delight, pleasing to the eye as well as being productive, but anyone who has attempted even a simple row of beans knows that a large vegetable garden means sustained effort over months, not days or weeks. It is fortunate, perhaps, that so many gardeners respond to the stimulus of competition.

I have always fancied myself as a vegetable gardener but even when I had a large vegetable patch there were vegetables that I did not consider worth the trouble. Shallots and broad beans are such easy vegetables that anyone with a sunny site and reasonably fertile ground should be able to manage them. Other than these, if I were going to grow just a few vegetables, I would make my priority a few rows of delicacies, such as crinkly Cos lettuce and infant turnips.

What I would always want in my garden is a good supply of herbs.

The modern cottage gardener can choose from among many spring-, autumn- and winter- flowering bulbs that all help to extend the flowering season.

Those I consider essential include parsley, thyme, chives, mint, tarragon (French not Russian), rosemary, borage, marjoram, sorrel and, last but not least, lovage.

Pursuit of an Ideal

When you asked me to contribute on this topic, I hunted out the following quotation from William Robinson. 'English cottage gardens are never bare and seldom ugly. Those who look at sea or sky or wood see beauty that no art can show; but among the things made by man nothing is prettier than an English cottage garden, and they often teach lessons that "great" gardeners should learn, and are pretty from snowdrop time till the Fuchsia bushes bloom nearly into winter. We do not see the same thing in other lands.' Robinson did not write as an impartial observer but he wrote with feeling of an ideal that still exercises a powerful influence on the minds of Englishmen.

The modern realization of that ideal is full of variations and contradictions. What is remarkable is that, despite great social and economic changes, so much of a long and simple tradition should survive with such vigour into our own day.

147

One Hundred Select Plants

Single measurements refer to the approximate height and spread of the mature plant, given reasonable growing conditions. When two measurements are given, the height is first, followed by the spread. Unless otherwise stated, plants are deciduous.

TREES AND SHRUBS

Artemisia arborescens 'Faith Raven'; 1m (3ft). Rounded growth habit; evergreen, silvery lace-like leaves; tiny yellow flowers in summer. Dry, poorish soil; sun.

Berberis temolaica; 2.5m (8ft). Arching stems; grey-green leaves, white beneath; pale yellow flowers in spring, followed by red fruit. Ordinary soil; sun or light shade.

Bupleurum fruticosum; 1.8m (6ft). Lax growth habit; evergreen or semi-evergreen; blue-green, leathery leaves; small yellow flowers in late summer. Poor, dry or chalky soil; sun.

Buxus sempervirens (common box); to 3m (10ft). Dense bush, easily clipped to shape; evergreen, small, dark green leaves; inconspicuous flowers in mid-spring. Well-drained soil; sun or shade.

Cercis siliquastrum 'Alba' (Judas trees); 6m (20ft). Bushy growth habit, but can be trained as a single-stemmed tree; racemes of white, pea-like flowers on naked stems in spring, followed by round, pale-green leaves. Deep, rich soil; sun and shelter.

Cornus alba 'Spaethii' (dogwood); 3m (10ft). Erect growth habit; bright red young stems; small white flowers in spring, followed by small white berries; leaves strongly variegated gold. Moist soils; sun or light shade.

Cotinus coggygria 'Foliis Purpureis' (smoke bush); 3m (10ft). Rounded growth habit; deep-purple leaves, turning green, then light red in autumn; insignificant flowers in summer, followed by attractive, fluffy flower stalks. Poor, well-drained soil; sun.

Cydonia oblonga (common quince); 4.5m (15ft). Architectural growth habit; dark green leaves, woolly beneath; white or pale pink flowers in spring; yellow fruit, suitable for preserves, in autumn. Rich soil; sun.

Elaeagnus angustifolia 'Caspica' (oleaster, Russian olive); 9m (30ft). Spreading, pendulous growth habit; willowy, semi-evergreen leaves, silvery beneath; small fragrant flowers in early summer, followed by yellow, sweet fruit. Light soil; sun.

Fatsia japonica 'Variegata' (Japanese fatsia); 1.8m (6ft). Large, glossy, evergreen deeply lobed leaves, tipped with white; tiny white flowers in autumn, followed by black berries. Well-drained soil; sun or semi-shade.

Hamamelis mollis 'Pallida' (Chinese witch hazel); 3m (10ft). Spreading habit; spidery, lemon-yellow, fragrant flowers on bare stems in winter; foliage yellows attractively in autumn. Neutral or acid moist soil; sun or light shade.

Lavandula angustifolia (*L. spica, L. officinalis*) (English lavender); 60cm x 1m (2 x 3ft). Mounded growth habit; aromatic, evergreen, grey foliage; spikes of lavender flowers in summer. Light, well-drained, soil; sun.

Magnolia stellata 'Water Lily' (star magnolia); 2.5m (8ft). Rounded growth habit; pale pink buds, then star-shaped white flowers on bare branches in early spring. Rich, moist, lime-free soil; sun.

Malus trilobata (flowering crab apple), 6 x 1.8m (20 x 6 ft). Erect growth habit; deeply lobed, maple-like leaves, good autumn colour; white flowers in spring, occasionally followed by red or yellow fruit. Ordinary soil; full sun.

Parrotia persica; 6m (20ft). Shrubby, spreading growth habit; pale, flaky bark; hazel-like leaves with excellent autumn colour; modest, red-stamened flowers in early spring. Rich, well-drained soil; sun or light shade.

Philadelphus 'Belle Etoile' (mock orange); 3m (10ft). Spreading habit; single white flowers blotched purple at the base, richly scented. Well-drained soil; sun or light shade.

Phlomis chrysophylla; 1m (3ft). Lax growth habit; sage-like young leaves tinged yellow; whorls of golden yellow flowers in summer. Well-drained, poor soil; sun.

Phormium tenax 'Purpureum' (New Zealand flax); 1.8m (6ft) Clump former; tough, evergreen, sword-like, brownish purple leaves; occasional spikes of dull red flowers; semi-hardy. Ordinary soil; full sun.

Prunus subhirtella 'Stellata' (*P.s.* 'Pink Star') (spring cherry); 6m (20ft). Tight clusters of large, single pink flowers in spring, followed by mid-green leaves. Well-drained soil; sun.

Sambucus racemosa 'Plumosa Aurea' (golden-leaved red-berried elder); 2.5 x 1.8m (8 x 6ft). Architectural growth habit; deeply indented yellow leaves; yellow flowers in spring; occasionally scarlet berries. Moist soil; sun or light shade.

Sarcococca humilis (sweet box); 60cm x 1m (2 x 3ft). Suckering habit; evergreen, glossy, dark-green leaves; small but heavily scented white flowers in late winter or early spring. Moist soils; sun or shade.

Sorbus 'Joseph Rock' (mountain ash): 8 x 4m (25 x 13ft). Erect growth habit; pinnate leaves with good autumn colour; white flowers in spring followed by clusters of creamy yellow, long-lasting berries. Moisture-retentive soil; sun or light shade.

Taxus baccata (common yew); 4.5m (15ft). Dense, much-branched bush or tree, easily clipped to shape; evergreen, dark green linear leaves, yellowish on reverse; flowers relatively inconspicuous but fruit red and fleshy. Almost any soil that is not waterlogged; dense shade or full sun.

Teucrium fruticans (shrubby germander); 1.8m (6ft). Loose growth habit; bright green, evergreen leaves, felted beneath; lavender flowers in summer; tender. Light, well-drained soil; sun.

SHRUB ROSES (See also Climbing Plants)
Unless otherwise stated, rich, free-draining soil and full sun are the optimum growing conditions.

Rosa 'Chinatown' ('Ville de Chine'); 1.2 x 1m (4 x 3ft). Floribunda-type modern shrub; upright growth habit; glossy leaves; very fragrant, double yellow flowers.

Rosa 'Fantin Latour'; 2.1 x 1.5m (7 x 5ft). Centifolia; upright growth habit; very fragrant, soft-pink double flowers, fading to pale pink, especially in bright sun; free flowering.

Rosa 'Frühlingsmorgen'; 2.1m (7ft). Modern shrub; arching growth habit; small grey-green leaves; scented clear pink flowers with creamy centres; repeats in autumn.

Rosa 'Grandpa Dickson' ('Irish Gold'); 60cm–1m x 60cm (2–3ft x 2ft). Hybrid tea; upright growth habit; glossy, dark-green leaves; fragrant, large, pale yellow flowers, flushed pink; long flowering.

Rosa 'Great Maiden's Blush'; 1.5m (5ft). Alba; thick, bushy growth habit; grey-green foliage; scented, soft pink, semi-double flowers; long lived.

Rosa 'Iceberg'; 1.5m (5ft). Floribunda; free-branching bushy habit; light green foliage; slightly fragrant white flowers; free-flowering and recurrent.

Rosa 'Madame Isaac Periere'; 2.1 x 1.5m (7 x 5ft). Bourbon; clusters of extremely fragrant, deep cerise-pink, double, cup-shaped flowers; recurrent, with good show in autumn.

Rosa moyesii 'Geranium'; 2.5m (8ft). Modern shrub; erect, arching, stems; single, crimson-red flowers, followed by large, bottle-shaped orange-red hips.

Rosa 'Roseraie de l'Hay'; 2.5m (8ft). Rugosa; dense growth habit; bright-green leaves, semi-double or double, fragrant wine-red flowers, fading to pale purple; long flowering season.

Rosa glauca; 1.5m (5ft). Species; arching, reddish-violet stems; grey-green leaves, tinged with purple; single pink, white-centred flowers, followed by dark-red hips.

PERENNIALS
Acanthus mollis 'Latifolius' (bear's breeches); 1.2 x 1m (4 x 3ft). Clump former; deeply divided, shiny leaves; spikes of white and mauve flowers in summer; long-lasting decorative bracts. Poor soil; sun.

Alchemilla mollis (lady's mantle); 45cm (18in). Clump former; soft green, hairy, slightly pleated leaves; sprays of tiny, yellow-green flowers in summer; self-seeds freely. Any soil; sun or light shade.

Astrantia maxima (masterwort); 60 x 30cm (2 x 1ft). Clump former; divided foliage; heads of starry, greenish-pink flowers in summer. Good moist soil; light shade or full sun.

Campanula carpatica (bellflower); 30 x 30cm (1 x 1ft). Clump former; toothed, bright green leaves; cup-shaped flowers in shades of blue or white in mid-summer. Well-drained fertile soil; full sun.

Convolvulus mauritanicus 30cm x 1m (3 x 1ft). Sprawler; invasive growth habit; small leaves; blue morning-glory flowers in summer; semi-hardy. Well-drained soil; sun.

Cynara cardunculus (cardoon); 1.8 x 1m (6 x 3ft). Clump former; deeply divided, silvery grey leaves; large purple thistle heads in summer. Poor, well-drained soil; sun.

Dianthus 'Dad's Favourite' (old-fashioned pink); 30 x 60cm (1 x 2ft). Grey-green linear foliage; white flowers laced purple, in mid-summer. Ordinary free-draining soil; full sun.

Dicentra spectabilis (bleeding heart, Dutchman's breeches); 60 x 45cm (24 x 18in). Clump former; divided, grey-green leaves and arching stems; hanging, rose-red, heart-shaped flowers with protruding white petals in late spring and early summer. Fertile, well-drained soil; sun or light shade.

Epimedium × ***rubrum*** (barrenwort); 23cm (9in). Spreading growth habit; heart-shaped leaves, bronze when young, turning green; attractive autumn tints; nodding crimson flowers in early spring. Rich soil; sun or light shade.

Eryngium alpinum (sea holly); 75 x 45cm (30 x 15in). Clump former; blue-green, heart-shaped foliage; blue, thistle-like flowers and silvery blue bracts in summer. Well-drained soil; sun or light shade.

Euphorbia characias wulfenii (spurge); 1m (3ft). Sub-shrub; spreading, architectural clumps of upright stems with evergreen, grey-green pointed foliage; heads of yellow-green flower bracts in spring. Poor, well-drained soil; full sun.

Fragaria vesca (Alpine strawberry); 23cm (9in). Evergreen leaves; carpet former; white flowers in spring and summer, followed by small edible berries. Rich soil;

semi-shade.

Gentiana asclepiadea (willow gentian); 90 x 60cm (3 x 2ft). Graceful arching stems with willow-like leaves; deep blue or white flowers in late summer. Moist fertile soil; light shade.

Geranium endressii 'Wargrave Pink'; 60cm x 1m (2 x 3ft). Clump former; dense, vigorous growth habit; elegantly divided, pale-green evergreen leaves; salmon-pink flowers in spring and summer. Ordinary soil; sun or light shade.

Geranium phaeum (mourning widow); 60 x 45cm (24 x 18in). Clump former; soft-green leaves; nodding, maroon-black flowers in late spring; self seeds. Ordinary soil; sun, light or deep shade.

Gunnera manicata 3m (10ft). Clump former; enormous, bristly palmate leaves on long stalks; slender brown flower spike in summer; semi-hardy. Deep, rich, moist soil, especially near water's edge; sun.

Helleborus lividus corsicus *(H. corsicus, H. argutifolius)* (hellebore); 60cm (2ft). Clump former; grey-green, veined, evergreen leaves; pale-green, cup-shaped flowers in late winter and early spring; short lived but self-seeds. Well-drained, fertile soil; sun or light shade.

Hosta sieboldiana 'Elegans'; 75 x 60cm (30 x 24in). Clump former; blue-grey, deeply veined leaves up to 30cm (1ft) across; pale lilac flowers in mid- to late summer. Fertile, moist soil; light shade or full sun.

Mellianthus major (honey flower); 2.4 x 1.8m (8 x 6ft). Sub-shrub with striking, blue-grey, pinnate, aromatic leaves; brownish red flowers in summer; semi-hardy. Poor, well-drained soil; sun.

Ophiopogon planiscapus 'Nigrescens' (mondo grass); 45cm (18in). Spreading growth habit; nearly black, evergreen, grassy, strap-shaped leaves; spikes of silvery pink flowers in summer. Well-drained soil; sun or shade.

Paeonia mlokosewitschii (peony, Molly the witch); 75cm (30in). Clump former; single, lemon-yellow flowers with golden anthers carried above grey-green foliage in spring; good autumn foliage colour. Rich, well-drained soil; sun or light shade.

Pulmonaria saccharata 'Marjory Fish' (lungwort); 30 x 60cm (1 x 2ft). Clump former; evergreen, marbled, heart-shaped leaves; pink flowers, later turning blue, in spring. Rich, well-drained soil; light shade.

Polygonatum x hybridum (Solomon's seal); 1m x 30cm (3 x 1ft). Spreading growth habit; arching stems with clusters of white bells hanging from leaf axils in summer. Rich, moist soil; light shade.

Polystichum setiferum 'Acutilobum' (soft shield fern); 60cm (2ft). Clump former; deeply divided evergreen fronds with bulbils on tips. Ordinary soil; shade.

Primula veris (cowslip); 23cm (9in). Clump former; clusters of lightly fragrant, small yellow nodding flowers in spring; self seeds. Heavy soil, especially chalky; sun or light shade.

Pulsatilla vulgaris (pasque flower); 30 x 30cm (1 x 1ft).

Fern-like leaves; silky buds opening to mauve flowers, though colour variable, in mid-spring; feathery seed-heads. Ordinary well-drained soil; full sun.

Viola labradorica 'Purpurea' (violet) 15 x 30cm (6 x 12in). Carpet former; heart-shaped, dark-green, purple-flushed leaves; small mauve flowers in spring; self-seeds freely. Well-drained soil; sun or semi-shade.

ANNUALS, BIENNIALS AND BULBS

Anemone nemorosa *'Allenii'* (wood anemone); 20cm (8in). Tuber; spreading growth habit; large, star-shaped, rich lilac-blue flowers, with darker undersides, in spring. Well-drained soil; light shade.

Cardiocrinum giganteum (giant lily); 1.8 x 1m (6 x 1ft). Bulb; heart-shaped leaves; white, trumpet-shaped flowers in summer, followed by attractive seed pods; short lived but bulbils usually produced. Deep, rich, well-drained soil; light shade.

Cheiranthus × allionii (Erysimum × allionii) 'Apricot Delight' Siberian wallflower; 45 x 30cm (18 x 12in). Biennial; bushy growth habit; scented, apricot-pink flowers in late spring and early summer. Rich soil, especially chalky; full sun.

Convallaria majalis 'Fortin's Giant' (lily of the valley); 23 x 30cm (9 x 12in). Tuber; spreading growth habit; broadly spear-shaped leaves; large, bell-shaped fragrant white flowers in spring, slightly later than species. Most soils; sun or light shade.

Crocus flavus (C. aureus); 10cm (4in). Bulb; yellow-orange flowers in late winter; garden forms sterile. Well-drained soil; sun or light shade.

Crocus speciosus; 10 to 15cm (4 to 6in). Bulb; lilac-blue flowers in autumn. Ordinary well-drained soil, can be naturalized in grass; full sun.

Cyclamen hederifolium (C. neapolitanum) 'Album'; 15 x 30cm (6 x 12in). Tuber; marbled, ivy-like leaves; nodding white flowers in autumn; self seeds. Well-drained soil; light or deep shade.

Cynoglossum amabile 'Bluebird' (Chinese forget-me-not); 45 x 30cm (18 x 12in). Can be grown as hardy biennial, hardy annual or half-hardy annual; pure blue, funnel-shaped flowers in summer; self seeds. Ordinary soil; sun or light shade.

Dierama pulcherrimum (wand flower, angel's fishing rod); 1.5m x 30cm (5 x 1ft). Bulb; grassy leaves; pink, nodding, bell-shaped flowers on wiry stems in late summer. Rich, moist soil; sun.

Digitalis purpurea 'Alba' (white foxglove); 1.2m x 60cm (4 x 2ft). Biennial; one-sided spikes of white flowers in summer; self seeds. Well-drained soil; sun.

Erythronium revolutum 'White Beauty' (dog's tooth violet); 30cm (1ft). Bulb; marbled, heart-shaped leaves; white, nodding, lily-like flowers in spring. Rich, well-drained soil; light shade.

Fritillaria imperialis 'Lutea Maxima' (crown imperial); 1.2m x 45cm (4ft x 18in). Bulb; cluster of lemon-yellow, nodding, bell-shaped flowers on tall stalks in spring. Rich, free-draining soil; sun.

Galanthus nivalis 'Viridi-apice' (snowdrop); 20 x 5cm (8 x 2in). Bulb; clump former; nodding, white, bell-shaped flowers, with green-tipped petals, in late winter and early spring. Well-drained soil; sun or light shade.

Galtonia candicans (summer hyacinth, spire lily); 1.2 x 30cm (4 x 1ft). Bulb; floppy, grey-green leaves; spikes of nodding, greeny white bell shaped, fragrant flowers in late summer. Rich, well-drained soil; sun.

Iris histrioides 'Major' (netted iris); 15 x 7.5cm (6 x 3in). Bulb; deep blue flowers, before leaves, in winter. Light, well-drained soil, especially chalky; sun and shelter.

Lavatera trimestris (L. rosea) 'Mont Blanc' (annual mallow); 1.8m x 45cm (6ft x 18in). Can be grown as hardy or half-hardy annual; shrubby growth habit; grey leaves; tall spikes of white, hollyhock-like flowers in summer. Light soil; sun.

Lilium regale (regal lily); 1 to 2m (3 to 6ft). Bulb; linear, deep green leaves; heads of trumpet-shaped, fragrant flowers, white on the inside, purplish on the outside, in mid-summer. Fertile, well-drained soil; full sun or light shade.

Matthiola incana 'Beauty' ('Beauty of Nice') (stock); 45cm (18in). Can be treated as hardy or half-hardy annual; bushy growth habit; spikes of very fragrant pink flowers in summer. Light, well-drained soil; sun.

Moluccella laevis (bells of Ireland); 60 x 30cm (2 x 1ft). Half-hardy annual; tall spikes of tiny white flowers with attractive, long-lasting green calyces. Most soils; sun.

Narcissus 'Peeping Tom' (daffodil) 40 x 7.5cm (16 x 3in). Bulb; fragrant, deep-yellow flowers in spring. Well-drained soil; sun or light shade.

Phlox drummondii 'Beauty Mixed' (annual phlox); 40 x 25cm (16 x 10in). Annual; rounded heads of self-coloured flowers in toning shades of red, pink, purple and white in summer. Well-drained soil; sun.

Scilla sibirica 'Multiflora' (Siberian squill); 20 x 5cm (8 x 2in). Bulb; pale-blue, dark-veined, nodding, bell-shaped flowers in late winter or early spring; self-seeds. Rich, well-drained soil; sun or shade.

Tulipa clusiana (lady tulip); bulb; 30cm (1ft). Single white flowers flushed with red, in mid-spring. Rich, well-drained soil; sun and shelter.

CLIMBING PLANTS

Actinidia chinensis (Chinese gooseberry; kiwi fruit); 9m (30ft). Twiner large, heart-shaped leaves; creamy white, fragrant flowers in summer followed by hairy, walnut-shaped fruit. Ordinary soil; sun or light shade.

Akebia quinata; 9m (30ft). Twiner; graceful, semi-evergreen leaves made of five leaflets; unusual, reddish purple, fragrant pendant flowers in spring. Ordinary soil; sun or shade.

Berberidopsis corallina (coral plant); 3m (10ft). Twining and scrambling evergreen; leathery leaves; clusters of small, dark-red drooping flowers in summer. Cool, moist, lime-free soil; semi-shade.

Clematis cirrhosa balearica (fern-leaved clematis); 3m (10ft). Evergreen with twining petioles; ferny leaves, turning bronze in winter; pale yellow flowers in winter, followed by silky seed heads. Cool, moist soil, especially chalk; sun.

Clematis 'Perle d'Azur'; 4.5m (15ft). Twining petioles; large, light-blue flowers in mid-summer. Cool, moist soil, especially chalk; sun.

Cobaea scandens 'Alba' (cathedral bells, cup and saucer vine); 3m (10ft). Semi-hardy perennial twiner, grown as a half-heady annual; greenish white bell-shaped flowers in summer, in green, saucer-like calyx. Ordinary soil; full sun.

Hedera colchica 'Paddy's Pride' (Persian ivy); 9m (30ft). Self-clinging evergreen; huge, heart-shaped, dark-green leaves centrally splashed with yellow, edged with pale green. Ordinary soil; sun or shade.

Humulus lupulus 'Aureus' (golden hops); 3m (10ft). Twining perennial with lobed yellow leaves; flowers not freely produced. Ordinary soil; sun.

Jasminum officinale 'Affine' (*J.o.* 'Grandiflorum') (summer jasmine); 9m (30ft). Semi-evergreen, twining climber; fern-like leaves; heavily scented large, white, trumpet-shaped flowers opening from pink buds in summer. Ordinary soil; sun or light shade.

Lathyrus latifolius 'White Pearl' *(L.l.albus)* (perennial pea); 3m (10ft). Perennial with twining tendrils; white, unscented, sweet-pea flowers in summer; dislikes extreme heat. Well-drained soil; sun.

Lonicera japonica 'Aureo-reticulata' (Japanese honeysuckle); 6m (20ft). Semi-evergreen twining climber; leaves with bright-yellow veins and midribs; fragrant white flowers, fading to yellow, in summer; semi-hardy. Cool, moist soil; sun and shelter.

Parthenocissus tricuspidata (Boston ivy); 15m (50ft). Self-clinging climber; large, lobed or heart-shaped leaves with rich crimson autumn colour; modest flowers in spring followed by dark-blue fruits. Well-drained soil; sun or light shade.

Rosa 'Aloha'; 3m (10ft). Climber; fragrant, rich pink flowers, fading to blush pink; repeat flowering. Rich, well-drained soil; sun.

Rosa 'François Juranville' 8m (25ft). Rambler; weeping growth habit; shiny green leaves, bronzy red when young; apple scented, rose-pink double flowers; slightly recurrent. Rich, well-drained soil; sun.

Tropaeolum speciosum (flame creeper); 4.5m (15ft). Twining perennial; scarlet flowers in mid- to late summer. Acid or neutral, well-drained soil; base in shade, top in sun.

Wisteria sinensis; to 30m (100ft). Vigorous twining climber; elegant leaves consisting of eleven leaflets fragrant mauve flowers in hanging racemes in late spring. Rich, well-drained soil; best flowering in full sun.

Gardens to Visit

NT signifies National Trust
P signifies Private

The North of England

Acorn Bank (NT), Temple Sowerby, Nr Penrith,
Cumbria
Old walled garden transformed into herb garden

Castle Howard (P), Coneysthorpe, North Yorkshire
Tel: Coneysthorpe 333
Classical landscape; 19th-century formal gardens; fine
collection of roses

Cragside House (P), Rothbury, Northumberland
Tel: Rothbury 20333
Moorland extensively planted with rhododendrons;
drives and walking tracks

Garden of 4 acres created since the mid–1950s; fine
lawns and island beds; many unusual plants

Canons Ashby (NT), Canons Ashby, Daventry,
Northamptonshire
Tel: Blakesley 860044
Formal gardens with terraces; large park

Chatsworth (P), Edensor, Derbyshire
Tel: Baslow 2204
Large landscaped garden with fine detailed planting;
modern greenhouse

Hare Hill (NT), Prestbury, Cheshire
Tel: Macclesfield 28855
Walled garden; good collection of rhododendrons

Howick Hall (P), Howick, Northumberland
Collector's garden with skilful informal planting

Levens Hall (P), Nr Kendal, Cumbria
Tel: Sedgwick 60321
Extraordinary topiary garden; ha-ha laid out in 1692;
large park with fine trees

Newby Hall (P), Skelton, North Yorkshire
Tel: Boroughbridge 2583
Garden covering 25 acres, redesigned since 1923;
features include handsome twin borders

Sizergh Castle (NT), Nr Kendal, Cumbria
Tel: Sedgwick 60070
Large rock garden; good collection of shrubs and
perennials

Wallington (NT), Cambo, Northumberland
Tel: Scot's Gap 283
Charming streamside garden

Central areas of England

Alton Towers (P), Nr Alton, Staffordshire
Tel: Oakamoor 702449
Extravagant romantic garden with fine trees, roses and
large rock garden

Arley Hall (P), Northwich, Cheshire
Tel: Arley Northwich 284
Old garden with sensitive modern planting; splendid
herbaceous borders

Barnsley House (P), Barnsley, Nr Cirencester,
Gloucestershire
Tel: Bibury 281
Old garden of 4 acres redesigned since 1960 with
formal and informal elements, including knot garden
and kitchen garden

Blenheim Palace (P), Woodstock, Oxfordshire
Tel: Woodstock 811325
'Capability' Brown landscape; formal gardens including
water parterre

Burford House (P), Tenbury Wells, Shropshire
Tel: Tenbury Wells 810777

Hardwick Hall (NT), Ault Hucknall, Derbyshire
Tel: Chesterfield 850430
Walled courtyard gardens with herbs, fruit and roses

Hidcote Manor (NT), Hidcote Bartram, Nr Chipping
Camden, Gloucestershire
Tel: Mickleton 333
Formal design created this century of hedged
enclosures richly planted; red border outstanding

Kiftsgate Court (P), Mickleton, Gloucestershire
Tel: Mickleton 202
Fine roses and shrubs, including tree peonies

Moseley Old Hall (NT), Moseley, Staffordshire
Tel: Wolverhampton 782808
Small garden designed in the 17th century style

Oxford Botanic Garden (University of Oxford),
Oxfordshire
Tel: Oxford 42737
The oldest botanic garden in Britain with many
interesting plants

Packwood House (NT), Packwood, Warwickshire
Tel: Lapworth 2024
Topiary gardens planted about 1650, said to represent
the Sermon on the Mount

Shugborough (NT), Great Haywood, Staffordshire
Tel: Little Haywood 881388
Landscape with many buildings in the neo-Grecian

style, and a Chinese pavilion; also 19th-century formal garden

Stone House Cottage Gardens (P), Stone
Nr Kidderminster,
Hereford and Worcester
Plantsman's walled garden

Tatton Park (NT), Knutsford, Cheshire
Tel: Knutsford 54822
Ornamental gardens, including a Japanese garden, and park

Eastern England

Anglesey Abbey (NT), Stow-cum-Quy,
Cambridgeshire
Tel: Cambridge 811200
Gardens covering 100 acres laid out this century; avenues of trees and sculpture

Belton House (P), Belton, Lincolnshire
Tel: Grantham 66116
Formal gardens and orangery; landscaped park

Beth Chatto Gardens (P), Nr Elmstead Market, Essex
Tel: Wivenhoe 2007
Dry garden, water garden and woodland garden made from an unpromising site since 1960; many unusual herbaceous plants

Blickling Hall (NT), Nr Aylsham, Norfolk
Tel: Aylsham 733084
In part 18th-century in design; splendid parterres and herbaceous borders laid out in the 1930s

Cambridge Botanic Garden (Cambridge University),
Cambridge, Cambridgeshire
Tel: Cambridge 50101
A teaching garden of considerable beauty; particularly interesting order beds

Felbrigg Hall (NT), Roughton, Norfolk
Tel: West Runton 444
Large gardens with fine lawns and shrubs; walled garden with flowers, fruit and vegetables

Hyde Hall (P), Rettenden, Essex
Roses and unusual trees and shrubs

Ickworth (NT), Nr Bury St Edmunds, Suffolk
Tel: Horringer 270
Formal gardens noted for fine trees

Oxburgh Hall (NT), Oxburgh, Nr King's Lynn, Norfolk
Tel: Gooderstone 258
Magnificent lawns, fine trees and borders and a parterre in the French style

London and the South of England

Ascott (NT), Wing, Nr Leighton Buzzard,
Buckinghamshire

Tel: Aylesbury 688242
Formal and informal gardens; topiary and lily pond

Borde Hill (P), Haywards Heath, West Sussex
Tel: Haywards Heath 50326
Many fine trees and shrubs in a woodland setting; herbaceous borders

Coates Manor (P), Fittleworth, West Sussex
Garden made since 1960 with the eye of a keen flower arranger

Cobblers (P), Mount Pleasant, Jarvis Brook,
Crowborough, East Sussex
Colourful garden of 2 acres with rich collection of shrubs and herbaceous plants

Cottesbrooke Hall (P), Nr Northampton, Hampshire
Formal and informal areas; features include herbaceous borders, Dutch and kitchen gardens

Denmans (P), Fontwell, Nr Arundel, West Sussex
Tel: Eastergate 2808
Designed and planted since 1946; informal groups of trees, shrubs and perennials, which are allowed to self-seed

Great Dixter (P), Northiam, East Sussex
Tel: Northiam 3160
An early 20th-century scheme, including yew topiary and hedges, with old and modern planting of exceptional quality

Hatfield House (P), Hatfield, Hertfordshire
Tel: Hatfield 62823/65159
Old garden with fine 20th-century planting, including parterres and roses; large park

Highdown (Worthing Corporation), Goring-by-Sea,
West Sussex
Tel: Worthing 204226
Richly planted garden created this century on chalk

Jenkyn Place (P), Bentley, Nr Farnham, Surrey
Gardens developed on old site since World War II; fine trees and shrubs, herbaceous borders and roses

Kew, The Royal Botanic Gardens, Kew, London
Tel: London 940 1171
Leading botanic garden with major scientific collections combined with very good ornamental planting

Leonardslee Gardens (P), Lower Beeding, Horsham,
West Sussex
Tel: Lower Beeding 212
Magnificent spring and autumn garden, with rhododendrons, camellias and magnolias

Mottisfont Abbey (NT), Nr Romsey, Hampshire
Tel: Lockerley 40757
Wall garden with major collection of old roses combined with herbaceous plants; other features include a knot garden

Nymans (NT), Handcross, West Sussex
Tel: Handcross 400321
Exceptional collection of plants, including camellias, eucryphias and magnolias, in 30-acre garden

Regent's Park, Queen Mary's Garden (Crown Property), London
Rose garden

Royal National Rose Society's Garden, Chiswell Green, St Albans, Hertfordshire
Tel: St Albans 50461/2
Large collection of roses, including trial beds

Savill Garden (Crown Property), Windsor Great Park, Berkshire
Tel: Windsor 68286
Outstanding 20th-century garden, richly planted

Scotney Castle (NT), Lamberhurst, Kent
Tel: Lamberhurst 890651
Highly romantic 19th-century picturesque garden with moated ruins as focal point

Sheffield Park (NT), Nr Uckfield, East Sussex
Tel: Danehill 790655
'Capability' Brown landscape superbly planted with trees and shrubs

Sissinghurst Castle (NT), Sissinghurst, Nr Cranbrook, Kent
Tel: Cranbrook 712850
Created by Vita Sackville-West and Sir Harold Nicolson from 1930 onwards; numerous elements linked in a complex design; outstanding collection of herbaceous plants

The Vyne (NT), Sherborne St John, Hampshire
Tel: Basingstoke 881337
Riverside setting; herbaceous borders, lawns and lake

Wakehurst Place (NT and Kew), Ardingly, West Sussex
Tel: Ardingly 892701
Magnificent collection of exotic trees, shrubs and herbaceous plants

Winkworth Arboretum (NT), Hascombe, Godalming, Surrey
Tel: Guildford 893032
A collection of trees and shrubs, many rare, covering nearly 100 acres

Wisley Garden (Royal Horticultural Society), Wisley, Nr Ripley, Surrey
Tel: Guildford 224234
Beautiful and instructive garden including model plots and trial grounds

The South-West of England

Abbotsbury Gardens (P), Abbotsbury, Dorset
Tel: Abbotsbury 387

Sub-tropical garden with many fine specimen trees

Barrington Court (NT), Nr Ilminster, Somerset
Tel: South Petherton 40601
Formal garden lavishly planted

Bicton Garden (P), Colaton Raleigh, Devon
Tel: Budleigh Salterton 3881
Formal garden in the French style, pinetum

East Lambrook Manor (P), East Lambrook, Somerset
Tel: South Petherton 40328
Cottage garden, formerly that of Margery Fish

Glendurgan (NT), Mawnan Smith, Cornwall
Tel: Bodmin 4281
Sheltered garden with many fine exotic trees

Killerton (NT), Broad Clyst, Devon
Tel: Exeter 881345
Early tree collection with good specimens of broad-leaved trees and conifers

Knightshayes Court (NT), Tiverton, Devon
Tel: Tiverton 254665
Young garden in an old setting; exceptionally attractive woodland

Lanhydrock (NT), Trebyan, Cornwall
Tel: Bodmin 3320
Main interest is the woodland planting of choice exotics

Montacute House (NT), Montacute, Somerset
Tel: Martock 823289
Grass, yew, old roses and perennials in harmony with the Elizabethan house

Stourhead (NT), Stourton, Wiltshire
Tel: Bourton (Dorset) 348
Classical landscape with many handsome trees

Tintinhull House (NT), Tintinhull, Somerset
Small garden of formal layout consisting of several enclosures, planted informally

Trelissick (NT), King Harry Ferry, Cornwall
Tel: Truro 862090
Beautifully situated woodland garden

Trengwainton (NT), Heamoor, Nr Penzance, Cornwall
Tel: Penzance 63120
Superb collection of exotic plants, many tender and sub-tropical

Tresco Abbey (P), Tresco, Isles of Scilly
Tel: Scillonia 849
Terraced gardens with sub-tropical plants

Westwood Manor (NT), Bradford-on-Avon, Wiltshire
Tel: Bath 64446
Modern topiary garden

Suggested Reading

This list attempts to strike a balance between the standard works of reference and the many fine books that convey a personal love and experience of plants and gardens.

Bean, W.G., *Trees and Shrubs Hardy in the British Isles*, John Murray, London, (8th edn) 1970 to 1980

Bowles, E.A., *My Garden in Autumn and Winter*, T.C. and E.C. Jack, Edinburgh, 1915, reprinted David and Charles, Newton Abbot, 1972 *My Garden in Spring*, T.C. and E.C. Black, Edinburgh, 1914, reprinted, David and Charles, Newton Abbot, 1972 *My Garden in Summer*, T.C. and E.C. Black, Edinburgh, 1914, reprinted David and Charles, Newton Abbot, 1972

Brookes, John, *The Garden Book*, Dorling Kindersley, London, 1984 *The Small Garden*, Marshall Cavendish Editions, London, 1977 *Room Outside*, Thames and Hudson, London, 1979

Chatto, Beth, *The Damp Garden*, Dent, London, 1982 *The Dry Garden*, Dent, London, 1978

Compton, James, *Success with Unusual Plants*, Collins, London, 1987

Crowe, Sylvia, *Garden Design*, Country Life, London, 1958

Fox, Robin Lane, *Better Gardening*, R & L, Beckley, 1982

Fish, Margery, *Carefree Gardening*, Faber & Faber, London, 1966 *Cottage Garden Flowers*, Faber & Faber, London, 1961

Gault, S.M. and Synge, P.M., *The Dictionary of Roses in Colour*, Ebury Press and Michael Joseph, 1971

Gibson, Michael, *Shrub Roses, Climbers and Ramblers*, Collins, London, 1982 *The Book of the Rose*, Macdonald and Jane, London, 1980

Hadfield, Miles, *A History of British Gardening*, John Murray, London, 3rd edn 1979

Hillier's Manual of Trees and Shrubs, David and Charles, Newton Abbot, 5th edn 1981

Hobhouse, Penelope, *Colour in Your Garden*, Collins, London, 1985 *The National Trust. A Book of Gardening: ideas, methods, designs. A Practical Guide*, Michael Joseph/Pavilion, London, 1986 *The Smaller Garden*, Collins, London, 1981

Jekyll, Gertrude, *Colour Schemes for the Flower Garden*, 1925, reprinted by Antique Collectors' Club, Woodbridge,

1982 *Wood and Garden: notes and thoughts, practical and critical, of a working amateur*, 1899, reprinted by Antique Collectors' Club, Woodbridge, 1981

Lloyd, Christopher, *The Adventurous Gardener*, Allen Lane, London, 1983 *The Well Chosen Garden*, Elm Tree Books, London, 1984 *The Well Tempered Garden*, Collins, London, 1970 *The Year at Great Dixter*, Viking, London, 1987

Page, Russell, *The Education of a Gardener*, Collins, London, 1962

Perry, Frances, *Collins Guide to Border Plants*, Collins, London, 1957 *The Observer Book of Gardening*, Sidgwick and Jackson, London, 1982 *The Water Garden*, Ward Lock, London, 1981

Phillips, C.E. Lucas, *The New Small Garden*, Collins, London, 1979

Reader's Digest Encyclopaedia of Garden Plants and Flowers, Reader's Digest Association, London, 2nd edn 1987

Robinson, William, *The English Flower Garden*, 1883, 15th edn with botanical revisions by G.S. Thomas, Hamlyn Publishing, Twickenham, 1986

Royal Horticultural Society, *Dictionary of Gardening*, Clarendon Press, Oxford, 2nd edn 1956 *The Fruit Garden Displayed*, Royal Horticultural Society, London, 5th edn 1974 *The Vegetable Garden Displayed*, Royal Horticultural Society, revised edn, 1970

Sackville-West, V., *The Illustrated Garden Book*, a new anthology edited by R.L. Fox, Michael Joseph, London, 1986

Scott-James, Anne, *Down to Earth*, Michael Joseph, London, revised edn 1981 *Sissinghurst*, Michael Joseph, London, 1975 *The Cottage Garden*, Allen Lane, London, 1981 and Sir Osbert Lancaster, *The Pleasure Garden: An Illustrated History of British Gardening*, John Murray, London, 1971

Stern, F.C., *A Chalk Garden*, Faber & Faber, London, 1960

Strong, Roy, *Creating Small Gardens*, Conran Octopus, London, 1986

Thomas, G.S., *Climbing Roses, Old and New*, Dent, London, revised edn, 1978 *Perennial Garden Plants*, Dent, London, revised edn 1982 *Plants for Ground-cover*, Dent, London, revised edn 1977 *Shrub Roses of Today*, Dent, London, revised edn 1974 *The Art of Planting*, Dent, London, 1984 *The Old Shrub Roses*, Dent, London, revised edn 1979

Index

Page numbers in *italic* refer to
illustrations

ACKNOWLEDGEMENTS

The Paul Press would like to thank the following photographers whose work appears in this book, plus the designers and owners of the featured gardens.

p.2 Jerry Harpur, **p.7** Jerry Harpur, **p.9** Pamla Toler (Impact Photos), **p.10** Jerry Harpur, **p.12** Hugh Palmer, **p.15** Jerry Harpur/Devigneol/ Simon Hornby, **p.17** Elizabeth Whiting, **pp.18–23** Richard Bryant, **pp.25–32** Jerry Harpur, **p.35** Eric Crichton, **pp.34–47 Jerry Harpur,** p.49 Jerry Harpur/Beth Chatto, **p.51** Hugh Palmer, **p.53** Jerry Harpur/Brook Cottage, Allerton, **p.54** Jerry Harpur, **p.57** Jerry Harpur, **p.58** Jerry Harpur, **p.60** Hugh Palmer, **p.63** Jerry Harpur, **p.65** Hugh Palmer, **p.66** Jerry Harpur, **p.68** Jerry Harpur/Jill Cowley, **p.71** Tania Midgley, **p.73** Jerry Harpur, **p.77** Hugh Palmer, **p.79** Jerry Harpur, **p.81** Hugh Palmer, **p.83** Jerry Harpur, **p.85** Jerry Harpur/Oon Drake, **p.86** Jerry Harpur, **p.88** Eric Crichton, **p.90** Jerry Harpur, **p.95** Hugh Palmer, **p.97** Tania Midgeley/Graham Thomas, **p.99** Jerry Harpur/Sissinghurst Castle, **p.100** Jerry Harpur, **p.103** David Joyce, **pp.105–111** Jerry Harpur, **p.112** Jerry Harpur/Windle Hall, St. Helens, **p.115** David Joyce, **p.117** Jerry Harpur, **p.119** Jerry Harpur/Abbots Ripton Hall, Cambs., **p.120** Eric Crichton, **p.123** Jerry Harpur/Brook Cottage, Allerton, **pp.125–28** Jerry Harpur, **p.130** Elizabeth Whiting, **p.133** Jerry Harpur, **p.135** Elizabeth Whiting, **p.136** David Joyce, **pp.140–44** Jerry Harpur, **p.145** Tania Midgeley, **p.147** Jerry Harpur, **p.149** Tania Midgeley